Critical framing of Žižek's work in his Balkan and Yugoslav context, as his repressed "maternal space," in order to test overall validity of his so-called radical political *praxis* is what distinguishes Homer's book from all other books on Žižek.
Dušan I. Bjelić author of Normalizing the Balkans. Geopolitics of Psychoanalysis and Psychiatry (2011).

Sean Homer shows the political value of a strict and profoundly antagonistic reading of Slavoj Žižek's work, a reading that does not shy from a necessary degree of interpretative violence to open up fissures in a body of work that pretends to be a system. With the context as the Balkans and crucial conceptual leverage provided by Alain Badiou, this radical scholarly book elaborates a distinctive argument in which violence is pitted against violence. Here we have a body of work as symptom laid bare, and through the course of the reading the reader can come to see more clearly how that symptom consists of a series of contradictions, speaks of a problem that it is not yet conscious of. Homer makes this symptom speak.
Ian Parker, Psychoanalyst, Manchester, Professor of Management, University of Leicester, UK.

SLAVOJ ŽIŽEK AND RADICAL POLITICS

In this book, Sean Homer addresses Slavoj Žižek's work in a specific political conjuncture, his political interventions in the Balkans. The charge of inconsistency and contradiction is frequently leveled at Žižek's politics, a charge he openly embraces in the name of "pragmatism." Homer argues that his interventions in the Balkans expose the dangers of this pragmatism for the renewal of Leftist politics that he calls for. The book assesses Žižek's political interventions insofar as they advance his self-proclaimed "ruthlessly radical" aims about changing the world. Homer argues the Balkans can be seen as Žižek's symptom, that element which does not fit into the system, but speaks its truth and reveals what the system cannot acknowledge about itself.

In Part II Homer explores Žižek's radicalism through his critique of Alain Badiou, arguing that Badiou's "affirmationism" provides a firmer grounding for the renewal of the left than Žižek's negative gesture analyzed in Part I. What distinguishes Žižek from the majority of the contemporary Left today is his valorization of violence; Homer tackles this issue head-on in relation to political violence in Greece. Finally, Homer defends the utopian impulse on the radical Left against its Lacanian critics.

Sean Homer is Professor of Film and Literature at American University in Bulgaria.

SLAVOJ ŽIŽEK AND RADICAL POLITICS

Sean Homer

Routledge
Taylor & Francis Group

NEW YORK AND LONDON

First published 2016
by Routledge
711 Third Avenue, New York, NY 10017

and by Routledge
2 Park Square, Milton Park, Abingdon, Oxon OX14 4RN

Routledge is an imprint of the Taylor & Francis Group, an informa business

© 2016 Taylor & Francis

Library of Congress Cataloging in Publication Data
Names: Homer, Sean, author.
Title: Slavoj Žižek and Radical Politics / Sean Homer.
Description: First published 2016. | New York, NY : Routledge, 2016. |
Includes bibliographical references and index.
Identifiers: LCCN 2016003533| ISBN 9781138643574 (hbk) | ISBN
9781138643581 (pbk)
Subjects: LCSH: Žižek, Slavoj. | Philosophy–Slovenia. | Nationalism–
Former Yugoslav republics.
Classification: LCC B4870.Z594 H66 2016 | DDC 199/.4973–dc23
LC record available at http://lccn.loc.gov/2016003533

ISBN: 978-1-138-64357-4 (hbk)
ISBN: 978-1-138-64358-1 (pbk)
ISBN: 978-1-315-62933-9 (ebk)

Typeset in Bembo
by Taylor & Francis Books

For Ella, Alice, James and Anneta

CONTENTS

COPYRIGHT

ACKNOWLEDGEMENT

Over the years I have benefited from many people's knowledge of Žižek's work and I can only mention a very few interlocutors here: Dušan Bjelić, Marios Constantinou, Nikolai Jeffs, Ian Parker, Ruth Parkin-Gounelas, Dragan Plavšić, Erica Sheen, Yannis Stavrakakis, Paul Stubbs. I would also like to thank Natalja Mortensen and Lillian Rand at Routledge for their assistance and advice. As always, all my remaining thanks go to Eugenie Georgaca.

PREFACE

This book is neither an introduction to Slavoj Žižek—there are more than enough of these already published—nor an account of Žižek's political theory—again there are a number of these already on the market and my differences with these accounts will be touched upon in the following chapters.

Rather, Part I of this book addresses Žižek's work in a specific political conjuncture: his political interventions in the Balkans. Unlike accounts of his political theory (Dean 2006; Johnston 2009; Sharpe & Boucher 2010; McMillan 2012), I do not try to extract a coherent political philosophy from Žižek's work or a particular strategy; indeed, I am not convinced on either account. Rather I address what Peter Osborne (2003) has referred to as Žižek's political journalism and how this plays out in his practice. The charge of inconsistency and contradiction is frequently leveled at Žižek's politics—a charge he openly embraces in the name of "pragmatism" (Žižek 2010, pp. 398–99), and it is my contention that his interventions in the Balkans expose the dangers of this pragmatism for the renewal of leftist politics for which he calls (Žižek 2009). There is a consistency to Žižek's politics within the Balkans over the past two decades. Unfortunately, the positions he does maintain are deeply conservative. In short, I take Žižek at his word that he is serious about changing the world and that his "ultimate aims are ruthlessly radical" (Žižek 2003, p. 503), and assess his political interventions insofar as they advance those aims.

Part II of the book takes its cue from Žižek's endorsement of Alain Badiou's "fundamental insight" that any radical emancipatory project today must pass through Lacan and go beyond Lacan. I contend, however, that any radical project today must pass through and go beyond Žižek, and from this perspective Badiou's work provides us with a more theoretically coherent position for the renewal of leftist politics. Once again, my focus is on Žižek's political interventions in the

Balkans, more specifically his support for the radical left in Greece and his endorsement of political violence—an issue that the majority of Žižek's commentators simply evade.

Like many Anglo-American academics, I started reading Žižek in the mid-1990s and was captivated by his unique ability to explicate Jacques Lacan through popular culture. More importantly, he appeared to bridge the gulf that post-Marxism had opened up between Lacanian psychoanalysis and Marxism. *The Sublime Object of Ideology* (1989) rehabilitated Marxian notions of ideology, commodity fetishism and surplus value that had been jettisoned by post-Marxist theories of discourse (Barrett 1991), and articulated a contemporary Marxist politics that was able to incorporate the insights of the Lacanian split subject. Political differences soon began to emerge, however. In the autumn of 1999 I read Žižek's response to the North Atlantic Treaty Organization (NATO) bombing of Serbia (Žižek 1999), or rather the first of his many responses, and became aware of how this response changed in relation to different audiences (Chapter 1). It appeared that there were very different "Žižeks," depending upon to whom he was speaking. I continue to find aspects of Žižek's work valuable, his analysis, for example, of the socio-ideological fantasy and his critique of nationalism as *das Ding* (the Thing). I am much less convinced by his contribution to the renewal of radical politics within Europe through notions of "revolutionary terror" and "strict egalitarian justice," or his attempt to rehabilitate "dialectical materialism" through a reading of Lacan.

In 1996 I published a rather modest conference presentation, "Psychoanalysis, Representation, Politics: On the (Im)possibility of a Psychoanalytic Theory of Ideology," in a small-circulation Lacanian journal. This paper was my first foray into the area of Žižekian-Lacanian-post-Marxist theory, and outlined a series of concerns I had with what was to me at the time new reading. Thanks to Yannis Stavrakakis's critique (Stavrakakis 1997, 1999), this paper has had a life far beyond anything I could have anticipated and has provided Žižekians with an exemplary case of misunderstanding the implications of Lacanian theory for political theory ever since. Such a critique appeared again recently in Chris McMillan's *Žižek and Communist Strategy* (2012). Following Stavrakakis, McMillan highlights my argument that the inability of Lacanian psychoanalysis to articulate a positive ideological position leaves it open to reactionary investments. With hindsight, and the steady shift of Lacanianism to the right,[1] I find myself even more convinced of this today than I was in 1996. Indeed, Žižek himself has become increasingly open in his criticism of the conservatism of orthodox Lacanianism and especially Jacques-Alain Miller's current desire to accommodate Lacanian psychoanalysis to social democracy (Žižek 2006, pp. 259–60). In *Less Than Nothing* (2012) Žižek argues that there is no psychoanalytic politics in the sense of a positive political program. The ultimate achievement of psychoanalysis has been to outline the contours of a "negativity," a disruptive force that undermines all collective projects. In short, psychoanalysis confronts us with a politics of the gap, the place where a political act can intervene, but paradoxically where "nothing is taking place but the place itself" (Žižek 2012, p. 963). From this perspective the relationship between psychoanalysis and politics is that of a parallax split, a missed encounter that is always too early or too late. For many Žižekians it is this recognition of the parallax gap and Žižek's steadfast refusal to offer a concrete alternative that is the mark of his radicalism (McMillan 2012, p. 94; Butler 2005, pp. 122–23).

As I argue below, the difficulty with maintaining such a position is that Žižek does "take sides" and many of these political stances do not live up to the radical rhetoric.[2] Žižek follows his discussion of the parallax gap with a sketch of the three basic positions one can adopt towards it: "a conservative-tragic celebration of the gap (we are ultimately doomed to fail ...), a liberal pragmatic assertion of the gap (democracy admits the imperfection of our societies ...) and the radical-leftist eternalization of struggle" (Žižek 2012, p. 964). From my perspective, if we are not to fall into either the tragic celebration that nothing can be done or the resignation that this is the best of all possible worlds, then we need to offer a positive alternative to these two positions. Here I am much more in agreement with the "Marxian Žižek" who argues that there can be no Lacanian politics as such:

> That is an extremely reactionary version, one in which politics is a neo-conservative sceptical resistance—the idea being that every new political project, if you take it too seriously, involves some new totalitarian closure. In this version, politics is the domain of ideological illusions, and psychoanalysis doesn't have a positive political project of its own, but instead allows you to keep open the gap, to maintain distance, so that you don't fall into the political trap. This kind of skepsis towards politics as such, which is very fashionable with some postmodern authors. I don't mean that when I say that there is no Lacanian politics. I only mean that, if you look at it historically, all attempts directly to formulate a Lacanian or psychoanalytic politics, all non-dialectical attempts to politicise psychoanalysis, have ended up in some sort of deadlock. I don't think that Lacanianism, even Lacanian psychoanalysis, can directly substitute for a proper Marxist social analysis.
>
> (Žižek 2000, p. 183)

Žižek continues that Marxists have put "too much false hope in psychoanalysis" (Žižek 2000, p. 184), hoping that it will provide the missing link to explain Marxism's failure, and this is a lost battle. What Lacanian psychoanalysis provides is a non-reductionist, but still materialist, theory of historically situated subjectivity. This is the Žižek I continue to find useful but there are, as we know, many other Žižeks out there.

Interestingly McMillan does not pursue Stavrakakis's main, and in part correct, criticism, that I am naively utopian (Stavrakakis 1997, pp. 115–16).[3] I do indeed believe that all creative socialist thought is likely to possess a utopian dimension (Anderson 1980, pp. 157–75), but, as I argue in Chapter 6, such a utopian fantasy does not imply the belief that the system can be harmonious and unified, and does not rule out the constitutive nature of negation. For Lacanians utopia is reducible to the fantasy of full jouissance and, once again, this is not the notion of utopia that runs through Western Marxism from Ernst Bloch to Fredric Jameson. McMillan does not pursue this line of argument because he also wants to retrieve the positive aspects of Žižek's utopianism. Our differences lie in the fact that McMillan contrasts Žižek's refusal to move beyond the negative, critical gesture inherent in the utopian impulse unfavorably with Jameson and Badiou, whereas, once again, I argue the opposite. I continue to believe that it is not enough, although it is absolutely necessary, for the radical left to be critical of global capital, that we must articulate positive alternatives if we wish to mobilize wider mass support. In short, we need an affirmative demand that we can universalize.

Notes

1 On the rightward shift of Lacanianism see Jacques-Alain Miller's dismal "The Politics of the Dream and the Politics of Desire" (2012), where he eulogizes on his love of country and French honor. See also Alain Badiou's discussion of the trajectory of his former associates at the *Cahiers pour l'Analyse* (Badiou 2012, pp. 289–90).
2 In this respect see Žižek's interventions in the debate on Syrian refugees and "Islamo-Fascism" (Žižek 2015a, 2015b).
3 I am not sure why Stavrakakis writes "quasi-utopian" here. I am simply utopian, but this is a much richer tradition of socialist thought than most Lacanians seem to be aware.

References

Anderson, P. (1980) *Arguments within English Marxism*. London: Verso.
Badiou, A. (2012) Theory from Structure to Subject: An Interview with Alain Badiou. In Hallward, P. & Peden, K. (eds) *Concept and Form, Volume Two, Interviews and Essays on the Cahiers pour l'Analyse*. London: Verso.
Barrett, M. (1991) *The Politics of Truth: From Marx to Foucault*. Cambridge: Polity Press.
Butler, R. (2005) *Slavoj Žižek: Live Theory*. London: Continuum.
Dean, J. (2006) *Žižek's Politics*. London: Routledge.
Homer, S. (1996) Psychoanalysis, Representation, Politics: On the (Im)possibility of a Psychoanalytic Theory of Ideology. *The Letter: Lacanian Perspectives on Psychoanalysis* 7: 97–109.
Johnston, A. (2009) *Badiou, Žižek and Political Transformations: The Cadence of Change*. Evanston, IL: Northwestern University Press.
McMillan, C. (2012) *Žižek and Communist Strategy: On the Disavowed Foundations of Global Capitalism*. Edinburgh: Edinburgh University Press.
Miller, J.-A. (2012) The Politics of the Dream and the Politics of Desire. *Hurly-Burly: The International Lacanian Journal of Psychoanalysis* 7: 267–270.

Osborne, P. (2003) Interpreting the World: September 11, Cultural Criticism and the Intellectual Left. *Radical Philosophy* 117: 2–12.

Sharpe, M. & Boucher, G. (2010) *Žižek and Politics: A Critical Introduction*. Edinburgh: Edinburgh University Press.

Stavrakakis, Y. (1997) On the Political Implications of Lacanian Theory: A Reply to Homer. *The Letter: Lacanian Perspectives on Psychoanalysis* 10: 111–122.

Stavrakakis, Y. (1999) *Lacan and the Political*. London: Routledge.

Žižek, S. (1989) *The Sublime Object of Ideology*. London: Verso.

Žižek, S. (1999) Against the Double Blackmail. www.balkanwitness.glypx.com (accessed 19 July 2013).

Žižek, S. (2000) An Interview with Beaumont, M. & Jenkins, M. *Historical Materialism: Research in Critical Marxist Theory* 7: 181–197.

Žižek, S. (2003) A Symptom—of What? *Critical Inquiry* 29 (Spring). pp. 486–503.

Žižek, S. (2006) *The Parallax View*. Cambridge, MA: MIT Press.

Žižek, S. (2009) *First as Tragedy, Then as Farce*. London: Verso.

Žižek, S. (2010) *Living in the End Times*. London: Verso.

Žižek, S. (2012) *Less Than Nothing: Hegel and the Shadow of Dialectical Materialism*. London: Verso.

Žižek, S. (2015a) The Non-Existence of Norway. *London Review of Books*. 9 September. www.lrb.co.uk/2015/09/09/slavoj-zizek/the-non-existence-of-norway (accessed 23 November 2015).

Žižek, S. (2015b) In the Wake of Paris Attacks the Left Must Embrace its Radical Roots. *In These Times*. 16 November. inthesetimes.com/article/18605/breaking-the-taboos-in-the-wake-of-paris-attacks-the-left-must-embrace-its (accessed 23 November 2015).

PART I
Žižek in the Balkans

INTRODUCTION

The case of Kosovo

It could be argued that the issues discussed in the first part of this book are dead and buried; in the words of Adrian Johnston, these "non-textual interventions and socio-political situations are long forgotten by everyone save for a few specialist intellectual historians and biographers" (Johnston 2009, p. xxii). So, why resurrect these debates yet again today?

The answer is simple. Žižek continues to return to these "socio-political situations" himself, he continues to attack what he perceives to be the position of the Western European left on the Balkans and these views are then recycled by his followers. In one of the earliest and most prescient critiques of Žižek, Peter Dews (1995) observed that there was a peculiar ambiguity in his political profile between "*marxisant* cultural critic on the international stage, member of the neo-liberal and nationalistically inclined governing party back home" (ibid., p. 26).

This became very apparent in 1999 when Žižek published a response to the North Atlantic Treaty Organization (NATO) bombing of Serbia (Žižek 1999a), or rather, the first of many responses, as his position changed depending upon whom he was addressing at the time (Chapter 1). Žižek continues to advocate a series of conservative political positions within the Balkans in contrast to the radicalism of his more widely disseminated texts and interviews. An adherence to the State, which in Žižek's own estimation differentiates him from all other manifestations of the radical left today, results in him continuing to support governments long after they have abandoned any pretense at radicalism. Indeed, over the intervening two decades the discrepancy between Žižek's domestic and international profiles has become more pronounced. Žižek has remained, to the best of my knowledge, completely silent on the violent anti-austerity protests in Slovenia in 2012, in marked contrast to his high public profile in Greece and immediate response to the more recent protests in Bosnia-Herzegovina in 2014

(Žižek 2014a, 2014b). Žižek, as we will see below, advances "pragmatic" solutions to the ongoing conflicts and crises in the Balkans, which he characterizes as getting his hands dirty and facing up to the realities of political power, in contrast to academic leftists. However, these solutions are often contradictory and at times indistinguishable from the right. It is conceivable that Žižek underwent an understandable, and even justifiable, conservative phase after the collapse of the Soviet Union and disintegration of Yugoslavia, and that he has now returned to his radical roots. If we consider the case of Kosovo, however, or his continuing support for SYRIZA (the Coalition of the Radical Left and Movements) in Greece (see the Introduction to Part II), this does not appear to be so. Despite the twists and turns of his thoughts on the Balkans there is an underlying consistency to his positions and these tend to be reactionary. The Balkans, in this sense, can be seen as Žižek's symptom, that element which does not fit into the system but speaks its truth and reveals what the system cannot acknowledge about itself. Let me now turn to the case of Kosovo.

The case of Kosovo

In 2013 Žižek co-authored a book with Agon Hamza entitled *From Myth to Symptom: The Case of Kosovo*. In their joint introduction the authors argued that the book goes to the core of the Kosovo problem by locating it with respect to two crucial political and ideological conjunctures: the NATO bombing of the former Yugoslavia in the late 1990s and the developments that followed thereafter. Furthermore:

> The underlying premise of these papers is that the occurrences in the former Yugoslavia, starting from its disintegration two [sic] the independence of Kosovo cannot be accounted for by any of the existing dominant paradigms that build their arguments around notions of ethnicity and culture.
> *(Žižek & Hamza 2013, p. 11)*

Žižek and Hamza argue, correctly I believe, that the neo-imperialist "universal values" being imposed upon Kosovo, such as democracy and multi-ethnicity, and the emergence of local nationalism are simply two sides of the same coin, and it is perhaps time to question what they call "democracy without the people" (Žižek and Hamza 2013, p. 14). The aim of the book is twofold:

> First, to break with the sophism of the post-modern tradition of de-politicising and culturalising the "case of Kosovo," as well as to break away from its supplement: that of the ethno-centric reasoning. Second, for the first time ever, it aims to provide a leftist reading of a country which has been subject to all sorts of (neo)imperial interventions and experiments.
> *(Žižek & Hamza 2013, p. 13)*

Leaving to one side the rather questionable claim that this is the first leftist analysis of the Kosovo question *ever*, we might ask what exactly the novelty of their approach is. Žižek and Hamza's alternative is to study what actually happened in the country and engage "in critical analysis of the existing state by rendering visible its limitations, inconsistencies and obscenities" (Žižek and Hamza 2013, p. 15). This all sounds fine until we turn to Žižek's actual contribution.[1]

Žižek's contribution, "NATO as the left hand of God," was first published over a decade earlier (Žižek 1999b), and it is reproduced here with a number of emendations. Žižek has changed references to the "Yugoslav democratic government" to "Serb 'democratic opposition'" (Žižek & Hamza 2013, p. 39), as if the two were simply the same thing and interchangeable. He has also added John Pilger (along with Tariq Ali and Alain Badiou) to his list of misguided leftists who opposed the NATO bombing, accusing Pilger and Badiou of inverted racism (ibid., pp. 22–23).[2] A large part of the essay is not directly related to the present situation in Kosovo at all; it is simply a cut and paste of material published elsewhere on Abu Ghraib and the "War on Terror." Finally, the more recent version drops the Bartleby solution to the problem which he advocated in 1999, as his faith in "do-nothing" politics seems to have waned.

Žižek's piece, thus, can be seen to offer us an analysis of the first of the two crucial political and ideological conjunctures, the NATO bombing of the former Yugoslavia in the late 1990s, and restates his longstanding position supporting and justifying NATO intervention, but it does not offer a "concrete" analysis of the situation in Kosovo today. It is not at all clear to me how this squares with Hamza's view of "strange leftist individuals" who support NATO (Žižek & Hamza 2013, p. 84, note 63), but I will leave that to one side. Žižek's ire, as always, is directed as much against the Western European left as the right, and his charge of racism against Pilger and Badiou is scurrilous. Pilger may, as Žižek points out (Žižek & Hamza 2013, p. 22), be wrong in this particular instance regarding the former Yugoslavia, but he is a figure of the left who has a long history of fighting racism within his own country, as does Badiou, and which sadly Žižek does not (see Chapter 3). Hamza pursues this line further:

> This is where the (Western) left got it wrong. It is all too easy to criticise the NATO bombing, indeed it was fashionable and almost everybody did it. In 1939 Max Horkheimer wrote "whoever is not prepared to talk about capitalism should also remain silent about fascism." The same should apply to the (Western) left: "whoever is not prepared to talk about the apartheid of the 90s [in the former Yugoslavia], should also remain silent about the NATO bombing."
> *(Žižek & Hamza 2013, p. 98)*

I am not sure where Hamza was during the late 1990s, but in the North of England, where I then lived, opposition to the NATO bombing was far from "fashionable." The demonstrations against the bombing were some of the smallest

I ever supported and, as I argue later, the left was deeply divided over the issue (Chapter 1). Furthermore, from my own experience, the left that opposed the bombing also supported the opposition movements in the former Yugoslavia, including Kosovo. There were surely some on the left who maintained illusions about the Milošević regime, but these were a minority.[3]

Žižek's contribution to the volume offers a robust critique of the depoliticization of the discourse of human rights and the logic of victimization, insofar as the ideal subject-victim is always a non-political subject. The ultimate paradox of victimization, he writes, is that "the other is good INSOFAR AS IT REMAINS A VICTIM" (Žižek & Hamza 2013, p. 32, emphasis in the original). It is this depoliticized discourse that both the humanitarian opposition to NATO and the left shared, and to which Žižek opposes his own solution:

> The way to fight the capitalist New World Order is not by supporting local proto-Fascist resistances to it, but to focus on the only serious question today: how to build TRANSNATIONAL political movements and institutions strong enough to seriously constraint [sic] the unlimited rule of the [sic] capital, and to render visible and politically relevant the fact that the local fundamentalist resistances against the New World Order, from Milošević to le Pen and the extreme right in Europe, are part of it.
>
> *(Žižek 1999b, n.p., emphasis in the original)*

This is entirely consistent with Žižek's position in 2013 (Žižek & Hamza 2013, p. 44), but what he leaves out of the reprinted version of the paper is his suggestion that the only viable solution for Kosovo is the ethnic partition of the country:

> To avoid any misunderstanding: the Albanian cleansing of the Serbs is to be unequivocally condemned and prevented—however, one should also make the next logical step and simply accept that, in the present situation of the ethnic hatred, the "cantonization" of Kosovo into an Albanian and a Serb part is the only viable solution.
>
> *(Žižek 1999b, n.p.)*

The question surely arises as to how we are to square this call for ethnic partition as the only viable solution with the first serious leftist critique that rejects the "ethnicization" and "culturization" of what is undeniably a political issue. Indeed, in 2001 Žižek repeated this argument word for word and praised the West for its "wise" decision to accept the *de facto* partition of Bosnia into three separate entities. This was not, however, a consequence of the ethnocentric reasoning of Western leaders but the result of their "nostalgic dream of the 'multiethnic' Yugoslavia; Kosovo is the last piece of the ex-Yugoslavia where this dream can still be enacted" (Žižek 2001). It is certainly possible, as I mentioned above, that Žižek's views have, not unreasonably, changed over the past decade, and his enthusiasm for ethnically divided states has been replaced by a belief in genuinely internationalist solidarity. However, from his public pronouncements this does not appear to be the case.

In a number of interviews that Žižek has given on the issue of the Balkans, including one with Hamza himself, he suggests that the only viable, pragmatic solution to Kosovo and the wider region is its partition into ethnically homogeneous states.[4] Shortly after the publication of *From Myth to Symptom*, Hamza conducted an interview with Žižek which addressed many of the issues covered in the book. Žižek's "logical" proposal to the "illogical," "disordered" and "unstable" solution of multiethnic states was:

> Here maybe foreign help is needed to prevent explosions. Why not give a little bit of that Mitrovica and so on [a Serb-dominated area in north Kosovo] to Serbia, maybe they can give you a little bit of the South-West of Serbia [where Albanians live] ... Wouldn't this be a much more, how to put it, a logical stable world. I think this problem is not insolvable [sic] in this sense. It can be done.
>
> *(Quoted in Plavšić 2014b)*

Žižek goes on to suggest the formation of a greater Albania[5] and the partition of Macedonia between a greater Albania and greater Bulgaria:

> If they [the Macedonians] really want, as I hear, some kind of unification with Bulgaria, then I would be brutal enough to say that this kind of restructuring of larger Albania, larger united Macedonia/Bulgaria, with all the necessary friendly, not brutally imposed, exchanges of territory with Serbia, what is bad about it, my God? I'm a pragmatic [sic] here.
>
> *(Quoted in Plavšić 2014b)*

Alternatively, we might ask, what is good about this solution? Like Plavšić, I have never heard any Macedonians express the wish to be unified with Bulgaria, but, be that as it may, why stop there? Approximately 25% of the Macedonian population is ethnically Albanian and one can only presume from Žižek's "brutal" logic that this part of the country will be united with a greater Albania along with Kosovo. There is also a significant Greek-speaking population in southern Albania, which can be united with a greater Greece, as the ethnically Turkish population of Greek Thrace can be reunited with Turkey and so on. Žižek seems already to have accepted the *de facto* ethnic division of Bosnia. Hamza addresses this response directly and asks Žižek if he is proposing ethnic states, to which he replies:

> No, I'm not for ethnically clean states. All I'm concerned about is how to create conditions for future coexistence. My God, listen, if there is a person who doesn't care about ethnicity ... it's me.
>
> *(Quoted in Plavšić 2014b)*

Again one has to ask, if Žižek's call for the acceptance of the *de facto* partition of Bosnia, a greater Albania and united Macedonia/Bulgaria is not a call for ethnically clean states, then what is it? Indeed, in an interview for *Al Jazeera Balkans* in 2012 he proposed exactly this: that Bosnia-Herzegovina be divided in two, with the Republika Srpska being annexed to Serbia. He went on to suggest that in exchange for the Serbian populated areas of Kosovo, Kosovo itself could be given parts of the Sandžak, an area on the Kosovo border that is currently divided between Serbia and Montenegro with a largely Bosniak (Bosnian Muslim) population. One can only wonder what the Montenegrins might think of this (Žižek 2013, quoted in Plavšić 2014f).[6] Indeed, I have no idea what the populations of these areas might think of these proposals, but then, as Žižek asks, "I, ok, who am I?" This would all be handed over to "the international community" to sort out in a "not brutally imposed" way. It would seem, therefore, that almost two decades after the NATO bombing of Serbia Žižek remains as committed to foreign intervention in the region as ever, but now under the guidance of that notoriously spurious entity "the international community."

Žižek's pragmatic solution for stability in the Balkans in 2012 is entirely consistent with the position he outlined in 1999 and 2001 regarding the "cantonization" of Kosovo and the partition of Bosnia along ethnic lines. There is nothing "ruthlessly" radical, as Žižek likes to say, about such a position; however, it is at once completely reactionary and highly problematic. If we look at the history of partitioned countries, from Ireland (1922), to India (1947), Cyprus (1974) and the Palestinian statelet of the West Bank and Gaza, we can see that such a solution hardly brings about peace and stability in a region (Plavšić 2014b). Furthermore, what form might a benign international intervention take? Is Žižek considering here an exchange of populations similar to what took place at the beginning of the twentieth century with the collapse of the Ottoman Empire?

If we return to the example of Ireland for a moment, and the signing of the Good Friday Agreement in 1998 which brought an end to major conflict in Northern Ireland we can see that it did not come about through benign intervention so much as a withdrawal of international players in the conflict.[7] In short, both the British state and the Irish Republic withdrew strategic interest and territorial claims respectively, and agreed to accept the will of the Northern Irish people as to the fate of their country. I am not suggesting that the Good Friday Agreement is ideal by any means but it does offer us an alternative to the false choice of "non-brutal" intervention or ethnically divided states.

Žižek's concrete proposals beg more questions than they answer and they are also starkly at odds with Žižek's position in the UK media on Bosnia, where he praises the recent protestors in Sarajevo for "expressing the will to ignore ethnic differences" (Žižek 2014a, 2014b). The pragmatic Žižek is also absent from his analysis of the conflict in Ukraine:

It's time for the basic solidarity of Ukrainians and Russians to be asserted, and the very terms of the conflict rejected. The next step is a public display of fraternity, with organizational networks established between Ukrainian political activists and the Russian opposition to Putin's regime. This may sound utopian, but it is only such thinking that can confer on the protests a truly emancipatory dimension.

(*Žižek 2014c, p. 37*)

I am completely in sympathy with Žižek's positions in both of these instances, but why can we not apply the same logic to the Balkans, rejecting the nationalist and neo-imperialist terms of the debate, along with the ethnocentric reasoning that divides the region into ethnically pure states, in favor of a "utopian" Balkan federation? Žižek's pragmatism, or what his critics usually identify as his political inconsistency, regarding the Balkans is not simply a matter of a non-textual intervention that will be long forgotten by everyone save for a few Balkan specialists and marginal left activists, but highlights a serious problem with his radical emancipatory politics that we must address, if we are not to fall into such reactionary scenarios as the "cantonization" of the region and calling in a benign international community to sort out our problems for us.

Notes

1 I focus on Žižek's essay here. Hamza's contribution "Beyond Independence" picks up from where Žižek leaves off and provides a much fuller account of the situation in Kosovo today.

2 The quotation and attack on Pilger can also be found in *The Year of Dreaming Dangerously* (Žižek 2012, p. 44, note 7).

3 The left has not completely ignored these events. Branka Magaš's (1989, 1993) account of the break-up of Yugoslavia commences with the student protests in Prishtinë in March 1981. By early April the protests had gathered momentum and were now demanding republic status for the Autonomous Province of Kosovo. On 3 April 1981 the Yugoslav People's Army entered the province and declared martial law for the first time since 1945.

4 I closely follow Dragan Plavšić's (2014a, 2014b, 2014c, 2014d) critique of Žižek in what follows. Hamza (2014) has written an *ad hominem* attack on Plavšić accusing him of spontaneous racism. I can only say that after a careful reading of Žižek's texts and viewing of the online interviews, I find Plavšić's criticisms to be well founded and textually supported.

5 "When you have Kosovo and Albania, the same nation, I mean, logically, there is no cultural tradition that would separate you and so on, I see nothing bad in thinking, why not unite the two" (Plavšić 2014b).

6 I was not able to verify this particular interview and once again rely on Dragan Plavšić's (2014f) account, as I have found his presentation of Žižek's words substantively correct in all other cases, so I see no reason for doubting his presentation here.

7 The armed struggle did not come to a complete end with the signing of the agreement. The Democratic Unionist Party initially opposed the agreement and sections of the Unionist paramilitaries did not start decommissioning their weapons until 2009.

References

Dews, P. (1995) The Tremor of Reflection: Slavoj Žižek's Lacanian Dialectics. *Radical Philosophy* 72: 17–29.

Hamza, A. (2014) A Response to Dragan Plavšić. *LeftEast*. 24 June. www.criticatac.ro/lefteast/a-response-to-dragan-plavsic/ (accessed 15 July 2014).

Johnston, A. (2009) *Badiou, Žižek and Political Transformations: The Cadence of Change.* Evanston, IL: Northwestern University Press.

Magaš, B. (1989) The Spectre of Balkanization. *New Left Review* (I) 174. pp. 3–31.

Magaš, B. (1993) *The Destruction of Yugoslavia—Tracking the Break Up 1980–92.* London: Verso.

Plavšić, D. (2014a) Did Somebody Say Ethnic Partition? A Critique of Žižek on Kosovo and the Balkans (Part 1). *LeftEast*. 9 June. www.criticatac.ro/lefteast/critique-of-zizek-on-kosovo-and-the-balkans-1/ (accessed 19 August 2014).

Plavšić, D. (2014b) Did Somebody Say Ethnic Partition? A Critique of Žižek on Kosovo and the Balkans (Part 2). *LeftEast*. 13 June. www.criticatac.ro/lefteast/critique-of-zizek-on-kosovo-and-the-balkans-2/ (accessed 19 August 2014).

Plavšić, D. (2014c) Did Somebody Say Ethnic Partition? A Critique of Žižek on Kosovo and the Balkans (Part 3). *LeftEast*. 16 June. www.criticatac.ro/lefteast/critique-of-zizek-on-kosovo-and-the-balkans-3/ (accessed 19 August 2014).

Plavšić, D. (2014d) Did Somebody Say Ethnic Partition? A Critique of Žižek on Kosovo and the Balkans (Concluding Part 4). *LeftEast*. 20 June. www.criticatac.ro/lefteast/critique-of-zizek-on-kosovo-and-the-balkans-4/ (accessed 19 August 2014).

Plavšić, D. (2014e) How Not to Debate: My Reply to Agon Hamza (Part 1). *LeftEast*. 2 July. www.criticatac.ro/lefteast/reply-and-appeal-to-hamza-and-lefteast-1/ (accessed 15 July 2014).

Plavšić, D. (2014f) How Not to Debate: My Reply to Agon Hamza (Concluding Part 2). *LeftEast*. 15 August. www.criticatac.ro/lefteast/last-plavsic-hamza/ (accessed 15 July 2014).

Žižek, S. (1999a) Against the Double Blackmail. www.balkanwitness.glypx.com (accessed 19 July 2013).

Žižek, S. (1999b) *NATO kao lijeva ruka Boga.* Zagreb: Arkzin.

Žižek, S. (2001) The Morning After. *Eurozine*. 27 March. www.eurozine.com/articles/2001-03-27-zizek-en.html (accessed 15 July 2015).

Žižek, S. (2012) *The Year of Dreaming Dangerously.* London: Verso.

Žižek, S. (2013) Kosovo Interview. 23 April. www.youtube.com/playlist?list=PLzCb-3H1Xd_U2L8MrE2AUh_t3Br_6MW5 (accessed 19 August 2014).

Žižek, S. (2014a) Anger in Bosnia, but this Time the People Can Read their Leader's Ethnic Lies. *The Guardian*. 10 February. www.theguardian.com/commentisfree/2014/feb/10/anger-in-bosnia (accessed 15 July 2014).

Žižek, S. (2014b) An Open Letter to the International Community in Bosnia and Herzegovina. *LeftEast*. 13 February. www.criticatac.ro/lefteast/an-open-letter-international-community-in-bosnia (accessed 15 July 2014).

Žižek, S. (2014c) Barbarism with a Human Face. *London Review of Books* 36(9). pp. 36–37.

Žižek, S. & Hamza, A. (2013) *From Myth to Symptom: The Case of Kosovo.* Prishtinë: Kolektivi Materializmi Dialektik.

1

IT'S THE POLITICAL ECONOMY, STUPID!

On Žižek's Marxism

> I have a very traditional Marxist belief that the new liberal-democratic order cannot go on indefinitely, that there will be a moment of explosion, probably caused by some kind of ecological crisis or whatever—and that we must prepare ourselves for that moment.
>
> *(Žižek 1996, p. 44)*

In a 1997 interview Slavoj Žižek was asked about the orientation of his recently commissioned series of books for Verso, *Wo es War*. He responded that while he had no overall plan for the series, its guiding principle was the rehabilitation of two orthodoxies. "The fact is," remarked Žižek, "that the strictly dogmatic Lacanian approach combined precisely with a not-post-Marxist approach is what is required today" (Žižek 1997, p. 133). Notwithstanding the rather coy reference to a "not-post-Marxist" approach here, Žižek's programmatic statement underscored an increasingly evident theoretical and political trajectory in his work—a trajectory that has spectacularly reversed his status as the most fashionable and mercurial theorist of the early 1990s to the *bête noir* of contemporary Cultural Studies. Žižek's recent polemics against post-Marxism, multiculturalism and identity politics have only served to highlight the distance that now exists between himself and his previous collaborators in the UK and US, Ernesto Laclau and Chantal Mouffe (Žižek 1999b, pp. 171–244; Butler et al. 2000).

As Peter Dews pointed out some time ago, Žižek has always maintained a peculiarly ambiguous political profile: "*marxisant* cultural critic on the international stage, member of the neo-liberal and nationalistically inclined governing party back home" (Dews 1995, p. 26). It seems to me, however, that the ambiguity of Žižek's position also extends to his international profile, as a postmodern, post-Marxist cultural critic one moment, orthodox Marxist the next. In this chapter I want to begin to untangle something of Žižek's ambivalent relationship with Marxism. For example, just how "orthodox" is Žižek's orthodoxy and, more importantly, how consistent is this position with a strictly "dogmatic" Lacanianism? Marxism, I suggest, has always been much more to the fore of Žižek's work than many of his commentators have cared to acknowledge, and his endorsement of post-Marxism has been equivocal at best. On the other hand, the precise nature of Žižek's Marxism has always been more difficult to fathom, while his thoroughgoing Lacanianism appears to rule out the possibility for any orthodox "understanding" of Marxism, or, indeed, the formulation of a clearly identifiable political project.

The formation of a global intellectual

It is difficult, I think, to underestimate the extraordinary success of Slavoj Žižek in Western European and North American academic circles, and yet it has never seemed evident to me why this should be so. Žižek's idiosyncratic hybrid of Hegelian dialectics, Althusserian Marxism and Lacanian psychoanalysis would not at first appear particularly congenial to an Anglo-American academic climate preoccupied with postmodernism, Queer theory and post-colonial studies. Jameson in *The Political Unconscious* (1981) is perhaps the only comparable figure who has tried to yoke together such theoretically incommensurable intellectual systems and he has been unremittingly criticized by the post-Marxist left for the attempt. A significant part in Žižek's overwhelmingly positive reception lies, to be sure, in his ability to tell a joke—more often than not the same one in different books. Significantly, the two early books that did more than anything else to popularize his work, especially *Looking Awry: An Introduction to Jacques Lacan through Popular Culture* (1991) but also *Enjoy Your Symptom! Jacques Lacan in Hollywood and Out* (1992a), are Žižek's least political works. Marx and Marxism do not figure prominently in either of these two volumes, and Žižek's facility to elucidate the notoriously impenetrable prose of Lacan through mainstream Hollywood film and genre fiction located him squarely with the postmodernists. The effortless shift from high theory to low culture and his undoubted love affair with North American popular culture have been crucial for his popularity. Žižek, as Robert Miklitsch writes, "appears to know the United States from the inside (as it seems only foreigners can do). This Žižek—the one we love to read because he reflects our own popular-cultural vision of the United States back to us (in reverse, as Lacan would say)" (Miklitsch 1998, p. 478). At least in terms of form, if not content, Žižek can be read as a thoroughgoing postmodernist and at times it would appear that Žižek himself has encouraged this reading of his work.[1]

The second and certainly politically more significant factor relating to Žižek's reception in the UK and the US was the ideological filter of post-Marxism. *The Sublime Object of Ideology* (1989), the first work of Žižek to be translated into English, was published in Laclau and Mouffe's series *Phronesis* which, as its opening statement makes clear, is committed to anti-essentialism, post-structuralist theory and a new vision for the Left conceived in terms of "a radical and plural democracy" (Laclau and Mouffe 1985, p. 176).

In a sense, Žižek's work could not have been translated at a more opportune moment. In Eastern Europe, the historic collapse of "actually existing socialism" and the break-up of the Soviet Union were gathering pace, while in Western Europe the final demise of Western Marxism seemed assured if not already complete. The intellectual currents of postmodernism and post-Marxism were at their most vitriolic and triumphalist. Any sense, for example, that Laclau and Mouffe remained within an essentially Marxian problematic, as with the conclusion of *Hegemony and Socialist Strategy* (1985), was expunged from their work (Laclau and Mouffe 1987). From *The Sublime Object* to *Looking Awry*, Žižek, the former dissident under "socialism" who also knew American popular culture better than most Americans, encapsulated the moment. It is hardly surprising, therefore, to see Žižek so unequivocally coopted to the banner of post-Marxism as in Laclau's "Preface" to *The Sublime Object*. Laclau situates the work of Žižek and the Slovenian school in relation to Lacanianism on the one hand and classical philosophy on the other, but with only a passing reference to Marx (as a philosopher) and the influence of a certain "Marxist-structuralist" theorist (Laclau 1989, p. x) and "Marxist currents" (ibid., p. xiv). Laclau concludes:

> For all those interested in the elaboration of a theoretical perspective that seeks to address the problems of constructing a democratic socialist political project in a post-Marxist age, it is essential reading.
>
> *(Laclau 1989, p. xv)*

Again, Žižek did much to encourage this view in interviews. As in a 1990 interview for *Radical Philosophy*, which took place on the eve of Slovenia declaring itself the first independent republic from the Federal Republic of Yugoslavia, and wherein Žižek discussed his position within the newly formed Slovene Liberal Democratic Party (Žižek & Salecl 1996). In contrast to the neo-liberalism dominant in the rest of Europe, the Liberal Democratic Party in Slovenia formed part of the opposition bloc and was closely aligned with the new social movements, in particular the feminist and ecological movements. What was distinctive about the Liberals, remarked Žižek, was their opposition to populist nationalism, a political tendency that united all the other major political groups, from the reformed communists and Greens to the far right. With their ideology of pluralism, ecology and the protection of minority rights, the Liberals saw themselves as drawing on a tradition of radical democratic liberalism. It is not difficult to discern here the post-Marxist agenda, insofar as it is articulated in Chantal Mouffe's *The Return of the Political* (1993), and according to which the goal of contemporary politics is not so much to overturn the structures of the state but to deepen and extend the reach of democratic practices and institutions. There is, however, one key area in which Žižek is in tune with neo-liberalism. Despite defining himself as a Marxist and locating the Liberal Democratic Party in opposition to free-market economics, he observes that with regard to economic restructuring he is a "pragmatist": "If it works, why not try a dose of it?" (Žižek & Salecl 1996, p. 31).

Specters of Marx

The absence of Marx and any acknowledgement of the positive value of a Marxian legacy in Laclau's "Preface" is interesting from the perspective of Žižek's own text. The first chapter of *The Sublime Object* is entitled "How did Marx invent the symptom?" and presents a sustained analysis of the commodity form, commodity fetishism, ideology, Althusser and surplus value. In psychoanalytic terms one might want to argue that there is a certain moment of repression taking place here, a sense that is confirmed if one turns to Žižek's "Introduction." *The Sublime Object* opens with a consideration of "proper names," or rather, the absence of certain names from Habermas's *The Philosophical Discourse of Modernity*. Lacan, notes Žižek, is mentioned only five times in this book and each time in conjunction with someone else—as with Marx in Laclau's "Preface". "Why this refusal," asks Žižek, "to confront Lacan directly, in a book that includes lengthy discussions of Bataille, Derrida and, above all, Foucault?" (Žižek 1989, p. 1). The answer to this enigma does not, as one would expect with Žižek, lie with Lacan himself but elsewhere; it lies with a name so deeply repressed in *The Philosophical Discourse of Modernity* as not even to be mentioned—that is to say, Althusser. The Habermas-Foucault debate, in other words, is masking another theoretically more far-reaching encounter between Althusser and Lacan:

> There is something enigmatic in the sudden eclipse of the Althusserian school: it cannot be explained away in terms of a theoretical defeat. – It is more as if there were, in Althusser's theory, a traumatic kernel which had to be quickly forgotten, "repressed"; it is an effective case of theoretical amnesia.
>
> *(Žižek 1989, p. 1)*

It may seem a little churlish to point out that Laclau and Mouffe's own theoretical formation was Althusserian-Marxist were it not for the fact that even at this early stage of their collaboration, Althusserianism is where Žižek and post-Marxism part company. Both Laclau and Mouffe's post-Marxism and Žižek's Marxism are grounded in the attempt to go *beyond* Althusser.

Beyond Althusserian interpellation

Laclau has always acknowledged certain differences of view with Žižek, for example, over whether or not Lacan is a post-structuralist and how one should read Hegel.[2] When Žižek began to formulate a more substantive critique of post-Marxism in 1990, however, this centered neither on Lacan nor Hegel but that enigmatic silence that surrounds Althusser. According to Žižek, Laclau and Mouffe's collaborative work of the 1980s marked something of a theoretical regression from their previous individual projects in one significant respect: that of the subject. The development of the notion of "subject positions" from *Hegemony and Socialist Strategy* onwards, argued Žižek, represented a step backwards from the more "finely elaborated Althusserian theory of interpellation" to be found in Laclau's earlier books (Žižek 1990a, p. 250). Theoretically, the notion of "subject positions" and the discursive constitution of identity remains locked within an essentially Althusserian problematic of ideological interpellation as constitutive of the subject. In short, "the subject-position is a mode of how we recognise our position of an (interested) agent of the social process, of how we experience our commitment to a certain ideological cause" (ibid., p. 251). Identification at this level conspicuously fails, as with Althusser's original theory of interpellation, to take into account that we are always-already subjects prior to the moment of interpellation.

"Strictly speaking," writes Žižek, "individuals do not 'become' subjects, they always-already *are* subjects" (Žižek 1994, p. 60). The question, therefore, is not as Althusser thought how we as individuals become subjects, but rather how we as always-already subjects become particular kinds of ideological subjects. What remains unthought in Althusser's theory is precisely this moment of interpellation prior to identification with the image. There is in a sense a kind of uncanny subject prior to subjectification, or, in more properly Lacanian terms, there is a void, a gap, at the core of the subject which "undermines the self-identity of the subject, with the subject itself" (ibid., p. 62). A direct consequence of this failure by Laclau to move beyond the Althusserian problematic of ideological interpellation, argues Žižek, is the theoretical eclipse of the most radical dimension of *Hegemony and Socialist Strategy*—that is to say, the notion of "social antagonism," or the very impossibility of the social to constitute itself as a stable unified totality. The whole notion of subject positions, contends Žižek, serves only to efface this fundamental traumatic experience and thus undermine the radical edge of post-Marxism.[3]

To put it another way, an anti-essentialist theory of fragmented subjectivity and multiple subject positions provides late capitalism with an intellectual justification for precisely that form of subjectivity most appropriate to meet the demands of a decentered, unstable and fluctuating global economy.

The critique of multiculturalism and identity politics

In the early 1990s Žižek's critique of the post-Marxist conceptualization of discourse and "subject positioning" turned on the question of the Lacanian notion of lack and antagonism. For Žižek, the crucial point rested upon whether or not the concept of antagonism represented an internal limit and fissure within the subject and the social itself—thus, to confront this limit was to confront the very impossibility of a coherent and unified system, or, alternatively, an external antagonism between already constituted subjects. As the latter route works within the pre-existing limits of the social it can be said to pose no real political threat at a systemic level. In his more recent work Žižek has spelled out the political consequences of subject positioning, multiculturalism and identity politics in rather less theoretical terms:

> since the horizon of social imagination no longer allows us to entertain the idea of an eventual demise of capitalism—since, as we might put it, everybody tacitly accepts that *capitalism is here to stay*—critical energy has found a substitute outlet in fighting for cultural differences which leave the basic homogeneity of the capitalist world-system intact. So we are fighting our PC battles for the rights of ethnic minorities, of gays and lesbians, of different lifestyles, and so forth, while capitalism pursues its triumphant march—and today's critical theory, in the guise of "cultural studies," is performing the ultimate service for the unrestrained development of capitalism by actively participating in the ideological effort to render its massive presence invisible: in the predominant form of postmodern "cultural criticism," the very mention of capitalism as a world system tends to give rise to accusations of "essentialism," "fundamentalism," and so on. The price of this depoliticization of the economy is that the domain of politics itself is in a way depoliticized: political struggle proper is transformed into the cultural struggle for recognition of marginal identities and the tolerance of differences.
>
> *(Žižek 1999b, p. 218)*

With echoes of Fredric Jameson, with whose work he has increasingly come to identify himself, Žižek now rails against the substitution of ethics for politics proper and the lack of utopian imagination that allows us to think beyond the limits of capitalism. Identity politics, he contends, is perfectly suited to our current depoliticized malaise, while multiculturalism is nothing less than the cultural expression of a consolidated global economy. The only way to combat postmodern particularism is through a (re)assertion of the dimension of universality and the messianic dimension of Marxism (Žižek 1999b, p. 142; Žižek 2000a). It is impossible today, argues Žižek, to remain impartial; to refuse to take sides is to support the global logic of capital, while, paradoxically, "accepting the necessity of 'taking sides', is the only way to be effectively *universal*" (Žižek 1999b, p. 223, emphasis in the original). What we are left with is, on the one hand, the retreat of radical democracy into liberalism and, on the other, the politics of the Third Way—that is to say, the politics of ideas that "work." Whereas the political act proper, contends Žižek, "is not simply something that works well within the framework of the existing order but something that *changes the very framework that determines how things work*" (Žižek 1999b, p. 199, emphasis in the original). This

Žižek is a long way from the liberal democratic "pragmatist" I mentioned earlier, who suggested in 1990 that if economic restructuring worked then Eastern Europe should try a dose of it.

Liberalism, or, Žižek's ambivalence

I have set out a reading of Žižek that depicts an almost linear progression from his early post-Marxist sympathies to his recent orthodoxy, but is Žižek really this "orthodox," and if this is the case, can all post-Marxists really be such poor readers? In 1990 Žižek published an article in the *New Left Review* on the disintegration of the former states of Eastern Europe and the rise of neo-nationalism (Žižek 1990b). Two years later he published a subsequent article in *New German Critique* entitled "Eastern European liberalism and its discontents" (Žižek 1992b). This second article was taken from the proceedings of a talk Žižek delivered at Columbia University.[4] In the first of these essays Žižek presented a compelling account of Western Europe's idealization and fascination with Eastern Europe in terms of Lacan's notion of *das Ding*, the Thing—that is to say, that elusive and unknowable Thing that is "something" only insofar as subjects constitute it as such. According to Žižek, the resurgence of ethnic violence and neo-nationalism within Eastern Europe did not represent a radical break from its immediate communist past but rather its continuation. In other words, the emergence of the "national-Thing" represents the return of the Real, the return of the traumatic kernel at the core of the social once the symbolic network of the communist ideology had disintegrated.

Žižek posed the question as to why the peoples of Eastern Europe would immediately re-impose such a repressive, intolerant and racist system if they had just overthrown the previous one. The answer to this question lies, not as Western commentators like to think, argues Žižek, in the primitive hatred and atavistic psychology of the people themselves, but rather in the logic of capital. "The elementary feature of capitalism consists in its *inherent structural imbalance*, its innermost antagonistic character: the constant crisis, the incessant revolutionizing of its conditions of existence" (Žižek 1990b, p. 59, emphasis in the original). As Žižek puts it, the rise of national chauvinism acts as a "shock-absorber" for this very excess of capital, and the inherent instability, openness and conflict that it introduces into the system. What we see in the violence and hatred unleashed in the Balkans, therefore, is not the re-emergence of ancient tribal hatred long suppressed by communism but the violence that underlies capitalism itself.

When Žižek was asked to address the same concerns but to a rather different audience at Columbia University, he began by characterizing the *New Left Review* article thus:

> The leftist demand to give a report on what is "really going on" in the East
> functions as a kind of mirror-reversal of this demand: we were expected to

confirm suspicions, to say that people are already disappointed in "bourgeois" democracy, that they slowly perceive not only what they have gained but also what they have lost (social security etc.). In my article, I consciously walked into this trap and gave the left what it wanted: a vengeful vision of how now things are even worse, how the effective result of democratic enthusiasm is nationalist corporatism—in short, it serves us right for betraying socialism!

(Žižek 1992b, p. 25)

Let me be clear here: Žižek does not reverse his original position on nationalism but rather takes the opportunity to underscore the *naïveté* of those "Third Way" dissidents—and one must presume that Žižek includes himself here—who believed there was an alternative to totalitarianism *and* capitalism. Along the way Žižek takes time to castigate Western Marxists whose "specialty" appears to be the ability to derive pleasure from the denunciation of nationalism which "is uncannily close to the satisfaction of successfully explaining one's own impotence and failure" (Žižek 1992b, p. 25). Now, certainly, we all speak to our audience, or as Jameson used to say, we speak in code, but what is troubling about this example from Žižek is the sense in which there is a deeper underlying logic at work here. Let me give another example, one politically more questionable.

In spring 1999 the *New Left Review* published a series of articles on the North Atlantic Treaty Organization (NATO) bombing of Yugoslavia, which included stringent critiques of NATO's action by Tariq Ali (1999), Edward Said (1999) and Peter Gowan (1999), as well as an article by Žižek entitled, "Against the double blackmail" (Žižek 1999c), which was highly critical of both NATO and the Serbs, especially Milošević's regime. Žižek's position on the bombing, as both anti-NATO and anti-Milošević, clearly holds a strong attraction for a Western European left which harbors no particular sympathy for either the former Yugoslavian president or NATO:

What if one should reject this double blackmail (if you are against NATO strikes, you are for Milošević's proto-Fascist regime of ethnic cleansing, and if you are against Milošević, you support the global capitalist New World Order)? What if this very opposition between enlightened international intervention against ethnic fundamentalists, and the heroic last pockets of resistance against the New World Order, is a false one? What if phenomena like the Milošević regime are not the opposite to the New World Order, but rather its *symptom*, the place at which the hidden *truth* of the New World Order emerges?

(Žižek 1999c, p. 79)

"Against the double blackmail" concludes with a brief plea for a "Third Way," not to be confused with the neo-liberal Third Way of Tony Blair and Bill

Clinton but a real Third Way of breaking "the vicious circle of global capitalism versus nationalist closure" (Žižek 1999c, p. 82). What is troubling about this article is that an earlier draft of it had been circulating on the Internet for some time prior to its publication in the *New Left Review*. This version is almost word-for-word identical to the published script, with the exception of its reassuringly "leftist" conclusion and one key sentence. Beyond the confines of the English-speaking world's leading Marxist journal, Žižek was not so measured in his solution to the problem of Milošević:

> So, precisely as a Leftist, my answer to the dilemma "Bomb or not?" is: not yet ENOUGH bombs, and they are TOO LATE.
>
> *(Žižek 1999a)*[5]

The reference here, as is clear from his subsequent paragraph, is Lacan's essay on *Hamlet* and the problem of logical time (Lacan 1981, 2006). What Žižek is alluding to is the impossibility of the Real as the inherent fissure and antagonism that underlies the social itself; in this sense, there can never be "enough" bombs to erase the trauma of the Real, and even if there were enough bombs, there would never be a right time to bomb as the encounter with the Real is always missed; one always arrives too early or too "late."

Yet, the sentence is strangely self-cancelling. What is the point of sending in more bombs if they will be too late anyway? For Žižek, therefore, the answer to the dilemma "bomb or not?" is apparently "yes and no!" From a psychoanalytic perspective one would want to say that there is something symptomatic about this statement in the sense that it unconsciously reveals what the author is quite consciously trying to hide. That is to say, there is a marked discrepancy between a sophisticated Lacanian understanding—that no amount of bombs at whatever time would be enough—and what we can call a naive or surface reading which would suggest that NATO should have gone in *harder* and *sooner*. The even-handed approach to a Third Way beyond global capital and totalitarianism has now gone and what we are left with is an insistence that NATO should have intervened against the Serbs earlier and more militaristically. The sentence is indicative of Žižek's apparent refusal to adopt an identifiable political position, yet at the same time it reveals in a symptomatic form the ambiguity of his politics due to his underlying nationalism. The uncomfortable fact that this is the *only* sentence removed from the Internet version of his paper suggests that Žižek was fully aware of its political reverberations, that there is a naive political reading of this sentence as well as a Lacanian one. Indeed, the sentence changes the whole tone of the piece and serves to highlight the anti-Serb nationalism that is evident in this article and so much of his recent writing on the Balkans (as I will discuss in the next chapter).

Let me briefly return to the long quotation on identity politics as an expression of the logic of global capital given above. Almost immediately following this quotation Žižek raises the possibility of a leftist response to the "falsity of multi-culturalist postmodernism," and here one might think we would find Žižek "taking sides" as he so stridently advocated. But no; the paradoxical conclusion to be drawn from this situation, observes Žižek, is that "today's true conservatives are, rather, leftist 'critical theorists' who reject both liberal multiculturalism and fundamentalist populism—who clearly perceive the complicity between global capitalism and ethnic fundamentalism" (Žižek 1999b, p. 221). In this instance we can safely read Judith Butler, Laclau and post-Marxism for "leftist," but what, one might legitimately ask, would be the alternative between liberalism and global capitalism if one has already accepted the failure of socialism? To paraphrase a comment by Ben Watson (1999), the question with Žižek is not whether or not to take him seriously but which one we should take seriously.

The return of the Real

Following on from their 1990 piece, *Radical Philosophy* conducted a second interview with Žižek in 1993, and it is illuminating to note the different tone of this later meeting. While he suggests that the political agenda of the liberal opposition is still to promote openness against the closure of nationalism, the old post-Marxist rhetoric of hegemony, articulation and discursive struggle has gone. Indeed, the whole notion of radical democracy is brought into question:

> This is why I am so suspicious of Laclau's concept of radical democracy, because basically it's simply a more liberal version of the standard liberal-democratic game—which is why he is uncannily silent about capitalism. That's his scarecrow.
>
> *(Žižek 1996, p. 37)*

Whereas previously Žižek had identified his oppositional stance with the new social movements, he now sees this as a distraction from the more pressing concerns of engaging with the contradictions and fundamental antagonisms of capital itself. Furthermore, while Žižek still at times accepts the legitimacy of identity politics—as long as we do not expect it to change anything fundamentally—at other times he argues that the creation of new forms of sexual subjectivity actively works against an emancipatory project and social transformation. "These Foucauldian practices," he notes, "of inventing new strategies, new identities, are [simply so many ways] of playing the late capitalist game of subjectivity" (Žižek 1996, p. 40). Following two civil conflicts in the former Yugoslavia, on the brink of a third and more brutal war in Bosnia Herzegovina, and after three years of economic restructuring, the subtle negotiation of identity, philosophy and culture in Žižek's work appears finally to have come up against the immovable rock of the Real, or, to put it another way, the economic logic of capital.

Marxism without Marx

The Real is something of a polysemous and migratory category in Žižek's work. It also marks the distance of his project from that of classical, or orthodox Marxism. In *The Sublime Object* the Real was explicitly aligned with Laclau and Mouffe's conception of *antagonism*:

> the precise definition of the real object: a cause which in itself does not exist—which is present only in a series of effects, but always in a distorted, displaced way. If the Real is the impossible, it is precisely this impossibility which is to be grasped through its effects. Laclau and Mouffe were the first to develop this logic of the Real in its relevance for the social-ideological field in their concept of *antagonism*: antagonism is precisely such an impossible kernel, a certain limit which is in itself nothing; it is only to be constructed retroactively, from a series of its effects, as the traumatic point which escapes them; it prevents a closure of the social field.
>
> *(Žižek 1989, pp. 163–64)*

We should keep in mind here that, as conceived by Laclau and Mouffe (1985, pp. 122–27), antagonism is to be clearly delineated from any Marxian conception of dialectical or determinate contradiction.[6] Žižek has also associated the Real with an Althusserian conception of history as an absent cause in his polemics against historicism:

> The symbolic order is "barred," the signifying chain is inherently inconsistent, "non-all," structured around a hole. This inherent non-symbolizable reef maintains the gap between the Symbolic and the Real—that is, it prevents the Symbolic from "falling into" the Real—and, again, what is ultimately at stake in this decentrement of the Real with regard to the symbolic is the Cause: the Real is the absent Cause of the Symbolic.
>
> *(Žižek 1994, p. 30)*

Finally, and most recently, the Real has come to be associated with the underlying logic of global capital itself. Reflecting on recent ecological crises in the introduction to *The Ticklish Subject*, Žižek remarks that "this catastrophe thus gives body to the Real of our time: the thrust of Capital which ruthlessly disregards and destroys particular life-worlds, threatening the very survival of humanity" (Žižek 1999b, p. 4).[7] The difficulty with Žižek's Marxism, however, arises precisely from his Lacanian conceptualization of the Real.

For Žižek, it is the Lacanian notion of the Real that separates his project from *both* post-Marxism and classical Marxism. If post-Marxism asserts the absolute irreducibility and particularity of political struggles to any single determining instance— the inherent contradictions of capital, for example—Lacanian psychoanalysis argues precisely the opposite. The multiplicity and particularity of contemporary struggles are, from a Lacanian perspective, a direct response to a single instance— that is, they are a response to the same impossible traumatic encounter with the Real.[8] However, can we say that this Real is a social contradiction in a Marxian sense? No! The Lacanian Real is not a Kantian "Thing-in-itself"; it is that which is beyond symbolization and too traumatic for the subject, or the social, to bear. The Real is essentially a gap, a void at the core of subjectivity and the social; it is a moment of impossibility that forestalls the unity of the subject and the cohesiveness of the social:

> The Real is therefore simultaneously both the hard, impenetrable kernel resisting symbolization *and* a pure chimerical entity which has in itself no ontological consistency ... the Real is the rock upon which every attempt at symbolization stumbles, the hard core which remains the same in all possible worlds (symbolic universes); but at the same time its status is thoroughly precarious; it is something that persists only as failed, missed in the shadow, and dissolves itself as soon as we try to grasp it in its positive nature.
>
> *(Žižek 1989, p. 169)*

According to Robert Miklitsch, the Real is in the final analysis a Hegelian pure "Thing-of-thought" (Miklitsch 1998, p. 486), but to emphasize the "ideality" behind the concept is to miss its inherent paradoxicality. The Real is both that which supports the symbolic order and at the same time that which undermines and disrupts it. As an absent cause it is also something that is retroactively con- stituted and the Marxian conception of the proletariat and class struggle function in precisely this way for Žižek.

Marxism's historic originality, contends Žižek, remains its identification of the structural role of class and class struggle as central to the logic of capital. While Laclau does not deny a role for class conflict per se, he does see this as only one possible subject position in a chain of potential identities and differences, and, moreover, one which is declining in importance in the contemporary world.[9] Žižek, on the other hand, argues that class struggle is not simply one social antagonism among a series of equally significant conflicts but "simultaneously the specific antagonism which 'predominates over the rest, whose relations thus assign rank and influence to the others. It is the general illumination which bathes all the other colours and modifies their particularity'" (Butler et al. 2000, p. 320). In other words, the very proliferation of political subjectivities and struggles today does not relegate class antagonism to a secondary role but they are the direct result of "class struggle" in the context of global capital.

Žižek's reassertion of the significance of class conflict in an era of globalization and the over-estimation of the politics of recognition is to be welcomed.[10] The "political" issues arise when we come to consider what he means by "class struggle" and whether or not this can have a *positive* formulation or simply represents "a certain limit, a pure negativity, a traumatic limit which prevents the final totalization of the social ideological field" (Žižek 1989, p. 164).

From a Lacanian perspective the subject is not an entity in itself but is rather the subject of the signifier; it is that which one signifier represents to another, or, to put it another way, it is a *breach* in the signifying chain (Fink 1995). Moreover, the subject can be seen to be constituted retrospectively; the subject comes into being, so to speak, as an answer to the question posed by the Real: "Why is there something rather than nothing?" Marx's formulation of the proletariat, suggests Žižek, provides a perfect example of this "substanceless subjectivity":

> the proletariat as the apogee of the historical process of "alienation," of the gradual disengaging of the labour force from the domination of the "organic," substantial conditions of the process of production (the double freedom of the proletarian: he stands for the abstract subjectivity freed from all substantial-organic ties, yet at the same time he is dispossessed and thus obliged to sell on the market his own labour force in order to survive).
>
> *(Žižek 1993, p. 26)*

Marx's mistake was to imagine that through the act of proletarian revolution a dialectical reconciliation of subject and substance could take place—that is to say, a process of dis-alienation and the full transparency of the process of production. Thus, in *Tarrying with the Negative*, Žižek provides a defense of Hegelian dialectics against the Marxian "materialist reversal" and argues that it is not Hegelian philosophy that is a closed, self-contained system but Marxism itself. What else, argues Žižek, is the Marxian conception of the proletariat if not the embodiment of this moment of closure, when the social is rendered in its entirety and self-transparent? Whereas Hegel's inscription of the negative at the very core of his system prevents any, one might say, ideological view of social transparency. Perhaps, writes Žižek, "after more than a century of polemics on the Marxist 'materialist reversal of Hegel', the time has come to raise the inverse possibility of a Hegelian critique of Marx" (Žižek 1993, p. 26). In short, Marx's critique of Hegel as an "absolute idealist" is nothing less than a displacement of his own disavowed ontology and is symptomatic of "the inherent impossibility of the Marxian project" (ibid., p. 26).

Class struggle: Yes and no!

For Žižek, the Lacanian Real is a moment of radical impossibility; it is that which will forestall all attempts at forging a unified coherent identity, and as such rules out the possibility of an orthodox Marxian response. The Real is the lack at the core of subjectivity and the void around which the social is structured, but as such it seems that it can be filled by anything. In Žižek's polemics with Butler and Laclau one can see how for the latter two, however much I disagree with their particular projects, the left constitutes and articulates a specific platform and political agenda. For Butler there is a need to engage in specific political struggles, even if they do not accord fully with one's theory, and not just debate the conditions of possibility for politics as such. Similarly, for Laclau, there is a need to engage in a Gramscian "war of position" to secure democratic gains. The difficulty with Žižek's position, suggests Laclau, "is that he never clearly defines what he understands by the global approach to politics" (Butler et al. 2000, p. 198). Moreover, his "discourse is schizophrenically split between a highly sophisticated Lacanian analysis and an insufficiently deconstructed traditional Marxism" (ibid., p. 205). Both Laclau and Butler insist on the need for Žižek to jettison the traditional Marxian conception of class and class struggle. I want to suggest to the contrary that it is Žižek's thoroughgoing Lacanianism that is the problem. It is his commitment to a Lacanian notion of the Real that rules out the possibility of giving his political project any positive content and thus reduces the political act to one of dissidence and opposition. Denise Gigante suggests that:

> Žižek is unique, and where he makes his radical break with other literary theorists who take up a position, any position at all that pretends to some notional content or critical truth, is in the fact that he fundamentally has no position.
>
> *(Gigante 1998, p. 153)*

In short, the point is to be anti-capitalist whatever form that might take. In the late 1980s for Žižek, this position was represented by liberalism and the new social movements, in the early 1990s by the possibility of ecological crisis, by the late 1990s it was opposing the logic of global capital, and now, with *The Fragile Absolute* (2000a), we find it is the "radical" legacy of Christianity.[11] This may be orthodox Lacanianism but it is hardly orthodox Marxism.

Notes

1 In a 1990 *Radical Philosophy* interview Žižek (Žižek & Salecl 1996) was challenged on Marx's distinction between those processes constituted by social recognition, such as money, and those beyond recognition, such as capitalist production. On this point, remarks Žižek, "I would be willing to describe myself as a 'postmodernist'" (ibid., p. 34). Earlier in this interview Žižek also favorably contrasts the postmodern acceptance of "a certain division of the price of freedom" (ibid., p. 24), with modernism's utopian vision of disalienation—a position starkly in contrast to his concluding statement in his exchange with Butler and Laclau, where Žižek strongly endorses a Jamesonian utopianism: "today's predominant form of ideological 'closure' takes the precise form of mental block which prevents us from imagining a fundamental social change, in the interests of an allegedly 'realistic' and 'mature' attitude" (Butler et al. 2000, p. 324).

2 The most sustained engagement between Laclau and Žižek on the position of Lacan in their work and their divergent readings of Hegel can be found in a series of point-by-point exchanges in their co-authored (with Judith Butler) book, *Contingency, Hegemony, Universality* (Butler et al. 2000). In brief, Laclau argues that Hegel's

system is a closed totality beyond which no further advance is possible and consequently it excludes contingency (ibid., pp. 60–1). Žižek, on the other hand, insists on the openness of the Hegelian dialectic through the mystery of "positing the presuppositions"—that is to say, the dialectical transformation of a contingent feature into the necessity of a structuring principle (ibid., pp. 227–28). For a critique of Žižek's "arrested" dialectic, see Dews (1995).

3 Žižek restated this position in *The Ticklish Subject* (1999b), where his critique of Badiou, Rancière, Balibar and Laclau turns on their common tendency to reduce the question of subjectivity to the process of subjectivization. As Žižek writes, "their theoretical edifices are to be conceived as four different ways of negating this common starting point, of maintaining (or, rather, gaining) a distance towards Althusser," but this is to miss the force of Althusser's original formulation: "subjectivization, of course, is not to be confused with what Althusser had in mind when he elaborated the notion of ideological (mis)recognition and interpellation: here subjectivity is not dismissed as a form of misrecognition; on the contrary, it is asserted as the moment in which the ontological gap/void becomes palpable, as a gesture that undermines the positive order of Being, of the differential structure of Society, of politics as police" (Žižek 1999b, p. 232).

4 A version of these two papers forms the final chapter of *Tarrying with the Negative: Kant, Hegel and the Critique of Ideology* (1993).

5 The first version of this article that I read was published at w2fd.hotmail.com/cgi-bin/ ge.G923730488.1&start+262297&len+45800. This version is no longer accessible online. A subsequent version published on the *Balkan Witness* website at www.balka nwitness.glypx.com (accessed 19 July 2013) cites the *New Left Review* article as its source but still contains the deleted sentence, the first sentence of paragraph 13. I would like to thank Ian Parker for his help in tracking down this source and Eugenie Georgaca for her suggestions.

6 "Antagonism, far from being an objective relation, is a relation wherein the limits of every objectivity are *shown* ... antagonism, as a witness of the impossibility of a final suture, is the 'experience' of the limit of the social. Strictly speaking, antagonisms are not *internal* but *external* to society; or rather, they constitute the limits of society, the latter's impossibility of fully constituting itself" (Laclau & Mouffe 1985, p. 125).

7 See also Žižek's critique of discursive relativism and historicism in *Contingency, Hegemony, Universality*: "today's real which sets a limit to resignification is Capital: the smooth functioning of Capital is that which remains the same, that which 'always returns to its place', in the unconstrained struggle for hegemony" (Butler et al. 2000, p. 223).

8 Judith Butler argues against Žižek's "universalization" of the Real in *Bodies that Matter: On the Discursive Limits of "Sex"* (1993), and restates this criticism in *Contingency, Hegemony, Universality* (Butler et al. 2000, p. 13).

9 See *Contingency, Hegemony, Universality*, wherein Laclau poses two "unassailable" arguments against the prioritization of social class: "(a) how do you know that these sets of descriptive features come together in some 'actually existing' social agents?; (b) even if you could point to empirical agents who would correspond to the Identikit of the 'working class', is not that very plurality of criteria showing already that the working class today is smaller than it was in the nineteenth century?" (Butler et al. 2000, p. 298).

10 Butler's argument against Žižek's prioritization of class struggle is illuminating for its narrowness of vision. It would seem that the pressing political concerns today are rolling back the frontiers of the state, gay marriage and gays in the military. There is no acknowledgement in Butler's intervention that this might be a specifically North American agenda, that other parts of the globe might have a rather different perception of the role of the state and civil society. When Butler does come to reflect upon European matters, the conflict in the Balkans for instance, we find a depressingly familiar

reiteration of NATO's line through the demonization of the Serbs and insistence on the legitimacy of the North American and Western European response.

11 This paper was completed before Žižek's writings on Trotsky and the legacy of Leninism (Žižek 2000b). I engage with Žižek's reading of Lenin in subsequent chapters and the conclusion below.

References

Ali, T. (1999) Springtime for NATO. *New Left Review* (I) 234. pp. 62–72.

Butler, J. (1993) *Bodies that Matter: On the Discursive Limits of "Sex"*. London: Routledge.

Butler, J., Laclau, E. & Žižek, S. (2000) *Contingency, Hegemony, Universality: Contemporary Dialogues on the Left*. London: Verso.

Dews, P. (1995) The Tremor of Reflection: Slavoj Žižek's Lacanian Dialectics. *Radical Philosophy* 72: 17–29.

Fink, B. (1995) *The Lacanian Subject: Between Language and Jouissance*. Princeton, NJ: Princeton University Press.

Gigante, D. (1998) Toward a Notion of Critical Self-Creation: Slavoj Žižek and the "Vortex of Madness". *New Literary History* 21(1): 153–168.

Gowan, P. (1999) The NATO Powers and the Balkan Tragedy. *New Left Review* (I) 234. pp. 83–105.

Habermas, J. (1987) *The Philosophical Discourse of Modernity*. Cambridge: Polity Press.

Jameson, F. (1981) *The Political Unconscious: Narrative as a Socially Symbolic Act*. London: Methuen.

Lacan, J. (1981 [1959]) Desire and the Interpretation of Desire in Hamlet. In Felman, S. (ed.) *Literature and Psychoanalysis, The Question of Reading: Otherwise*, Baltimore, MD: Johns Hopkins University Press.

Lacan, J. (2006 [1945]) Logical Time and the Assertion of Anticipated Certainty: A New Sophism. In Fink, B. (trans.) *Écrits*. New York: W.W. Norton & Co.

Laclau, E. (1989) Preface. In Žižek, S., *The Sublime Object of Ideology*. London: Verso.

Laclau, E. & Mouffe, C. (1985) *Hegemony and Socialist Strategy: Towards a Radical Democratic Politics*. London: Verso.

Laclau, E. & Mouffe, C. (1987) Post-Marxism without Apologies. *New Left Review* (I) 166. pp. 79–106.

Miklitsch, R. (1998) "Going through the Fantasy": Screening Slavoj Žižek. *Psycho-Marxism: Marxism and Psychoanalysis Late in the Twentieth Century, The South Atlantic Quarterly* 97(2): 475–507.

Mouffe, C. (1993) Radical Democracy: Modern or Postmodern. In *The Return of the Political*. London: Verso.

Said, E. (1999) Protecting the Kosovars? *New Left Review* (I) 234. pp. 73–75.

Watson, B. (1999) The Tamagochi and the Objet Petit a. *Radical Philosophy* 97: 42–44.

Žižek, S. (1989) *The Sublime Object of Ideology*. London: Verso.

Žižek, S. (1990a) Beyond Discourse Analysis. In Laclau, E., *New Reflections on the Revolution of Our Time*. London: Verso.

Žižek, S. (1990b) Eastern Europe's Republics of Gilead. *New Left Review* (I) 183. pp. 50–62.

Žižek, S. (1991) *Looking Awry: An Introduction to Jacques Lacan through Popular Culture*. Cambridge, MA: MIT Press.

Žižek, S. (1992a) *Enjoy Your Symptom! Jacques Lacan in Hollywood and Out*. London: Routledge.

Žižek, S. (1992b) Eastern European Liberalism and its Discontents. *New German Critique* 57: 25–49.

Žižek, S. (1993) *Tarrying with the Negative: Kant, Hegel and the Critique of Ideology*. Durham, NC: Duke University Press.

Žižek, S. (1994) *The Metastases of Enjoyment: Six Essays on Woman and Causality*. London: Verso.

Žižek, S. (1996) Postscript. In Osborne, P. (ed.) *A Critical Sense: Interviews with Intellectuals*. London: Routledge.

Žižek, S. (1997) Interview with Andrew Long and Tara McGann. *JPCS: Journal for the Psychoanalysis of Culture & Society* 2(1): 133–137.

Žižek, S. (1999a) Against the Double Blackmail. www.balkanwitness.glypx.com (accessed 19 July 2013).

Žižek, S. (1999b) *The Ticklish Subject: The Absent Centre of Political Ontology*. London: Verso.

Žižek, S. (1999c) Against the Double Blackmail. *New Left Review* (I) 234. pp. 76–82.

Žižek, S. (2000a) *The Fragile Absolute—or, Why is the Christian Legacy Worth Fighting For?* London: Verso.

Žižek, S. (2000b) Repeating Lenin. www.lacan.com/replenin.htm (accessed 1 July 2010).

Žižek, S. & Salecl, R. (1996) Lacan in Slovenia: Slavoj Žižek and Renata Salecl. Interview with Dews, P. & Osborne, P. In Osborne, P. (ed.) *A Critical Sense: Interviews with Intellectuals*. London: Routledge.

2

NATIONALISM, IDEOLOGY AND BALKAN CINEMA

Re-reading Kusturica's *Underground*

Throughout the 1990s Žižek advanced an incisive critique of the ideological fantasy structuring emergent neo-nationalisms in the Balkans. Deploying the Lacanian notions of the "theft of enjoyment" and *das Ding* (the Thing), Žižek persuasively described the construction of national differences between the Slovenes, Serbs and Bosnians. From a Žižekian perspective the national-Thing presents a privileged site of the eruption of enjoyment in the social field. Nationalism is nothing less than the manner in which subjects organize their enjoyment in relation to the Thing. Ethnic conflicts are essentially conflicts over the possession of the Thing and the belief that others have stolen it from us (Žižek 1990, p. 53). This analysis of nationalism as the theft of enjoyment also went hand in hand with a critique of Western Europe's response to the conflicts through the notion of the impotent gaze. First formulated by Lacan in his seminar on "The Purloined Letter" (2006), the impotent gaze can see what is taking place before it but is unable to act or intervene without compromising or implicating itself. In this sense, the conflict in Bosnia-Herzegovina acutely raised the issue of the "guilt of the gaze"; as Western Europe was reduced to a position of a pure impassive gaze that sees events unfolding before it and was utterly unable to do anything about it. The gaze, however, is never the gaze of the subject but the gaze of the object. What is at stake here is not so much the gaze of the West but the way in which that gaze is returned to us in its inverted form. "The true passive observers," writes Žižek, "are the citizens of Sarajevo themselves, who can only witness the horrors to which they are submitted without being able to understand how something so horrible is possible" (Žižek 1994, p. 214). This is the gaze that makes us feel guilty, the gaze that undermines our humanitarian, compassionate and civilized self-image. A third element in Žižek's critique of the Western European response to the conflicts in the former Yugoslavia was a scathing indictment of

Western liberal multiculturalism and leftist fascination with the Bosnian film director Emir Kusturica, in particular his 1995 film *Underground: Once Upon a Time There Was a Country*. It is here, I believe, that we can see the limits of Žižek's critique of neo-nationalisms and the presence of what I described previously as Žižek's anti-Serb nationalism but, for reasons that will become clear below, I think should more properly be called anti-Slav nationalism.

In *The Fragile Absolute* (2000), Žižek accuses Kusturica's Western European audiences of "reverse racism" (p. 5), a charge that he increasingly levels at anyone who disagrees with his positions on the Balkans. In *On Belief* (2001) he criticizes Kusturica for his "choice" of adopting a Serbian identity over his Bosnian one (p. 28).[1] Kusturica's epic tale of Yugoslav history from the 1940s to the 1990s was widely acclaimed by many Western European critics and won the Palme d'Or at Cannes, an award that elicited a vitriolic attack from the philosopher Alain Finkielkraut in the pages of *Le Monde*:

> In recognizing *Underground*, the Cannes jury thought it was honouring a creator with a thriving imagination. In fact, it has honoured a servile and flashy illustrator of criminal clichés. The Cannes jury highly praised a version of the most hackneyed and deceitful Serb propaganda. The devil himself could not have conceived so cruel an outrage against Bosnia, nor such a grotesque epilogue to Western incompetence and frivolity.
>
> *(Quoted in Iordanova 2001, p. 117)*

Kusturica had accepted partial funding for the film from Radio-Television Serbia and his critics attacked the film as simply Serbian government propaganda. A key point of contention was the use of documentary footage portraying Slovenes in Maribor and Croats in Zagreb cheering and welcoming Nazi troops in contrast to the devastation wrought on Belgrade by Nazi bombers, the fairly obvious implication being that the Croats and Slovenes were collaborators while the brave Serbs resisted the occupation. I will come back to this below. Kusturica defended his use of this documentary footage, arguing that he was trying to counter the selective humanism of the West in showing only the Serbs as the aggressors. He was, he insisted, against ethnic cleansing of all kinds, whether it came from Bosnians, Croats or Serbs.

Žižek's intervention in this debate came in a short article entitled "Underground, or Ethnic Cleansing as a Continuation of Poetry by Other Means" (1997a), which also appeared as a section in *The Plague of Fantasies* (1997b), in his influential essay "Multiculturalism, or, the Cultural Logic of Multinational Capitalism" (1997c), and briefly in "The Military-Poetic Complex" (2008). He took as his starting point not so much the film itself as the political controversy surrounding it and Kusturica's own, often unfortunate, response to the criticism. The political meaning of *Underground*, argued Žižek, "does not reside primarily in its overt tendentiousness, in the way it takes sides in the post-Yugoslav conflict—heroic Serbs versus the treacherous, pro-Nazi Slovenes and Croats—but, rather, in its very 'depoliticized' aestheticist attitude" (Žižek 1997c, p. 37). Žižek supported this argument with reference to an interview Kusturica gave in which he claimed that the film was not political at all but a "deferred suicide" note for the Yugoslav state. For Žižek:

> What we find here [in *Underground*] is an exemplary case of "Balkanism," functioning in a similar way to Edward Said's concept of "Orientalism": the Balkans as the timeless space onto which the West projects its phantasmatic content. Together with Milcho Manchevski's *Before the Rain* (which almost won the Oscar for the best foreign film in 1995), *Underground* is thus the ultimate ideological product of Western liberal multiculturalism: what these two films offer to the Western liberal gaze is precisely what this gaze wants to see in the Balkan war—the spectacle of a timeless, incomprehensible, mythical cycle of passions, in contrast to decadent and anaemic Western life.
>
> *(Žižek 1997c, p. 38)*

Žižek acknowledges that *Underground* is a multilayered and self-referential film but immediately dismisses this as postmodern cynical ideology. What Kusturica unknowingly provides us with, concludes Žižek, is "the libidinal economy of ethnic slaughter in Bosnia: the pseudo-Bataillean trance of excessive expenditure, the continuous mad rhythm of drinking-eating-singing-fornicating," or ethnic cleansing as poetry by other means (Žižek 1997c, pp. 39–40). Žižek continues by drawing a parallel between Kusturica and that other infamous Serbian nationalist poet Radovan Karadžić but, as Dušan Bjelić (2005) argues, this is rather "a hard sell" and paraphrasing Sartre's comment regarding "lazy Marxists" he writes "Yes, Kusturica, like Karadžić, poeticises 'the wild Serb man' but not every 'wild Serb' is Kusturica; yes, Karadžić is a poet, like Kusturica, but can Karadžić make [*Underground*]?" (ibid., p. 119, note 29). The problem with *Underground*, according to Žižek, is not that it is "political propaganda" but that it is *not* political enough.

Žižek is right, I think, on a number of counts. Kusturica is clearly a filmmaker who is playing to Western audiences. He is now more popular abroad than at home and his films deliberately exploit an aesthetics of self-exoticization taking up Western European clichés of the Balkans and playing them back to us in exaggerated form. Indeed, one could argue here that, similarly to Žižek's often repeated example of political resistance, Laibach, Kusturica is adopting a strategy of "over-identification," and thus by completely identifying with Western stereotypes he reverses the Western gaze (Gocić 2001, p. 84). Indeed, as we will come to see in the next chapter, after his break with Laibach and the *Neue Slowenishe Kunst* (NSK) Žižek has come to celebrate the Sarajevo *New Primitivs*, of which Kusturica's band, "The No Smoking Orchestra," was an integral part, as an exemplary form of cultural politics. This only serves to highlight for me the very problematic nature of such a political strategy—what one critic (Gocić) can take to be the ironic over-identification with Western stereotypes and myths, another (Žižek) takes to be the unconscious ideological fantasy of the director. How one is to distinguish between the two remains unclear.

The cyclical narrative structure of *Underground*—The War, The Cold War, War—is also, as Žižek points out, ideologically loaded, replicating Western European views of the Balkans as an atavistic, barbaric space outside time and history. I want to argue here, though, that it is the very multilayered and self-referential aspect of this film, which Žižek so quickly dismisses, that *is* the whole point of the film and not simply some cynical ideological ploy on the director's part. There is clearly a politics to *Underground* but not where Žižek is looking for it. The political aspect of this film lies in its form rather than its content. The problem here, as Sarah Kay highlights, is that Žižek reverts to the very kind of ideological interpretation of film for which he criticizes other theorists (Kay 2003, pp. 71–2). In short, Žižek does not read film as film but merely as an expression of the director's "unconscious" ideological fantasy, and in so doing reveals more of his own ideological position than he intended.

Underground as historical reconstruction

Underground, as I said above, represents the history of modern Yugoslavia from 1941, the outbreak of World War II, to 1992 and Bosnian conflict. The narrative is divided into three parts: The War (1941–); The Cold War (1961–); War (1992–). Each of these dates represents key moments in Yugoslav history: 1941—the dismemberment of the old Yugoslav state and the beginning of the partisan resistance; 1961—the first formal meeting of the Non-Aligned Movement in Belgrade and the opening up of Yugoslavia to the West; 1992—the Bosnian conflict and effectively the end of the Yugoslav state. This history is told, though, through the personal histories of the three main characters: two resistance fighters and communist party members, Marko (Miki Manojlović) and Blacky (Lazar Ristovski), and Natalija (Mirjana Joković), an actress and sometime mistress of Blacky and Franz (a Nazi officer) and later wife of Marko. After being informed on for stealing an arms shipment, Marko hides Blacky and his relatives in a cellar for the duration of the war but then tricks them into believing the war is still continuing and keeps them there for over 20 years. The lives of these three main characters are shown to be inextricably bound up with the history of the country but we are never left in any doubt that this is a very selective view of history, and history itself is contested.

Underground is a very self-conscious cultural artifact. Kusturica is a distinctively postmodern filmmaker in terms of his films' self-reflexivity, his use of parody and above all through his representation of history. This is not just a film about the history of a country that no longer exists but also, to borrow the dedication from another controversial film on the Bosnian conflict, a film about "the film industry of a country that no longer exists."[2] *Underground* constantly draws attention to itself *as* film and as the production of a specific film industry.[3]

I have already mentioned Žižek's comparison of Kusturica to Radovan Karadžić and there is a sense in which this comparison works in *Underground* but not in relation to Kusturica himself. The comparison is more appropriately applied to Marko, the Communist Party functionary who hides the partisans in the cellar in the first place and then keeps them imprisoned there. As well as being an international arms smuggler, Marko is an appalling nationalist poet and something of a stage director himself. Marko manipulates the partisans into remaining hidden in the cellar and believing that World War II is still going on through a complex theatrical charade. He constructs an elaborate *mise-en-scène*, through newsreels, music, bombing raids and special performances by his actress wife, Natalija. Marko in fact writes the scripts that he and Natalija will perform in front of the partisans in the cellar—scripts that constantly glorify Marko's own historical role but invariably involve her being humiliated and abused by the Nazis. This postmodern relativization of truth and representation is consistently emphasized within the film, especially in relation to Marko. If we are supposed to take Marko as exemplary of the brave Serbian nation then we also have to accept that he is a fraud from beginning to end. It is here, then, in relation to Marko as a character that Žižek's comparison to Radovan Karadžić as a poet and ethnic cleansing as a continuation of poetry by other means has resonance, and not to Kusturica as director. Given the explicitly deceitful and manipulative nature of this particular character, however, this would suggest that the film is a critique of such nationalist poets rather than an apology for them.

In the opening scene of part two (The Cold War), Marko is opening a cultural center in memory of his old friend and national hero Petar "Blacky" Popara, and he takes the opportunity to recite another of his poems. Poet, stage director, scriptwriter and actor, it would appear that Marko is something of a renaissance man were it not for the fact that he is a complete charlatan and motivated solely by self-interest. The character of Marko also serves to draw attention to the existence within the film of a range of cultural forms and genres. Most obviously there is the film within the film but also a play within the film and the montage sequences of archival documentary footage. This combination of different genres again highlights the issue of representational truth or, more properly in Žižekian terms, the "symbolic fiction" that masks the Real of social antagonism. Reality, for Žižek, is never directly "itself," it is only ever a failed symbolization that arises from the gap that separates reality from the Real. It is the function of ideology to render invisible this gap between social reality and the Real. It is also precisely this gap between the "symbolic fiction" of nationalist mythology and the Real of history that *Underground* renders visible.

Documentary is conventionally understood to be the opposite of a feature film. A documentary presents us with "real" information and historical facts; it aims at the truth rather than the imaginative reconstructions of fiction films. What happens, therefore, when these two genres are combined in a single artifact? Does the inclusion of documentary footage provide historical legitimacy for the fictional account, or does the fictional account undermine the veracity of the documentary presentation? As can be seen from the conflicting interpretations of *Underground*, it clearly does both. What is notable in *Underground* is the very diversity of ways in which this footage is incorporated into the film. There are scenes in the film where the documentary footage is simply spliced in, such as the bombing of Belgrade in 1941 or the controversial scenes of cheering grounds in Maribor and Zagreb. The archival footage has frequently been tinted so that we are aware that this material has been touched-up and manipulated. The documentary footage is also used very crudely and obviously as back projection, while in other instances Marko is seamlessly edited into sequences with Tito—we see Marko apparently shaking hands with Tito or standing with him on a balcony watching a 1 May parade. The overall effect of this diversity and integration of archival footage and fictional characters is to stress, yet again, the way in which film can be used, and has been used, in the reconstruction of Yugoslav history and national mythology. The gap between the representation and history itself is always explicit.

History as repetition: From tragedy to farce

Marx once wrote, paraphrasing Hegel, that all great events of history and world historical figures occur twice, "the first time as tragedy, the second as farce" (Marx 1973 [1869], p. 146).[4] The idea of history as repetition is most conspicuously evident in the central section of *Underground*, "The Cold War." Part two is all about the making of a film, but not just any film—it is the film of part one. The film within the film is a World War II partisan movie entitled *Spring Comes on a White Horse* and based on Marko's own memoirs of his "dead" friend and comrade Petar Popara (aka Blacky). The scene we see being filmed is Blacky and Natalija's wedding on a boat containing stolen arms. In contrast to the first time we see this scene, Marko is shown heroically defending the arms shipment while Blacky is captured trying to rescue Natalija and then executed. Marko and Natalija are invited onto the set to give the film their official stamp of approval and we are presented with the image of Marko (Miki Manojlović) first embracing an actor (Lazar Ristovski) playing the character of Blacky (Lazar Ristovski) and subsequently the actor (Miki Manojlović) who plays the character of Marko (Miki Manojlović), while Natalija (Mirjana Joković) kisses the actress (Miki Manojlović) who plays the character Natalija (Mirjana Joković), all the time commenting on how lifelike the actors look. The situation deteriorates even further when the "real" Blacky emerges onto the film set and starts to kill the cast of German soldiers, believing the war still to be going on. In this play of mirror images where performance and reality, truth and fiction, past and present become blurred, what we should not forget is that what is being rewritten is history itself, both in terms of the film's diegesis (Marko's memoirs), but also in relation to *Underground* as a text.

A film industry that no longer exists

The parody of partisan films is more than simply farce. Partisan films were one of the principal and most popular genres produced by this film industry that no longer exists. The classical period of Yugoslav partisan films was between the end of World War II and the early 1950s, what is usually referred to as the Red Wave. In the 1960s a new generation of film directors, the most well known in the West being Dušan Makavejev, reworked the genre into more personal and ambiguous visions of the past, much as Hollywood directors of the 1980s have done with the Vietnam War.[5] What was known at the time as New Yugoslav cinema but has posthumously been labeled "Black Film" or the "Black Wave" was particularly critical of the ultra-realism and kitsch of the Red Wave. After the political clampdown across Yugoslavia in the early 1970s there was a revival of Red Wave films.

Originally, partisan films served purely propaganda purposes, idealistically glorifying and confirming a revolutionary past and at the same time reinforcing this revolutionary spirit in the heroic struggle to construct a socialist society out of the ruins of the war. Partisan films also represented a particular national aesthetic, "nationalist realism," which Tito's government promoted as an alternative to the "socialist realism" of the Soviet Union. These films were technically crude, stereotypical and simplistic. The film-within-the-film, *Spring Comes on a White Horse*, is a classic partisan film in its low production values, stereotypical characters and over-dramatization, and could be read merely as a parody of the genre, except that the actual "historical" events upon which it is supposedly based, and which we saw in the first part of *Underground*, are no less a critique of the genre and the history that it represents. This is at once a nostalgic homage to a film industry that no longer exists and foregrounds the complicity of that film industry in the construction of historical memory and national mythology. Without wishing to labor the point, if *Underground* is in any sense a propaganda film, it is because it is a film *about* propaganda films.

This brings me to my second critique and the issue of spectatorship and reception. In his general antipathy to Cultural Studies, Žižek has never taken on board one of its central lessons concerning the ideological critique of cultural texts—that is to say, that we must take into account spectator agency and acknowledge the diversity of potential readings of and responses to any given text. In this sense Žižek is close to figures from the Frankfurt School, such as Adorno and Marcuse, from whom he otherwise wishes to distance himself.[6] Žižek tends to homogenize Western European audiences not acknowledging the divergence between a liberal academic, which I take to be humanist, and a leftist reading of *Underground*, which is more properly political. The wars in the former Yugoslavia, as I have argued previously, were deeply divisive for the European left and there was no unified "Western gaze" that somehow encompassed the left, just as there was no unified reception of *Underground* on the left. For his own polemical purposes against Cultural Studies, multiculturalism and what he sees as an academic left, Žižek posits a naive and passive audience and does not allow for the possibility of more negotiated and critical readings. We are all simply dupes of an unconscious Balkanism or reverse racism and unable to read the film for ourselves. One can appreciate, I think, the multilayered complexity of Kusturica's *Underground* and at the same time be critical of it—for instance, of its gender politics, which Žižek tends to ignore (see Longinović 2005, pp. 40–43). One can see the film as a critique of the myth of Tito's Yugoslavia and at the same time as a product of Yugo-nostalgia. That *Underground* is a fundamentally "contradictory" text is what makes it one of the more interesting productions attempting to come to terms with the break-up of the former Yugoslavia and its history.

Nesting orientalism and the return of the repressed

The issue of reception is crucial when we come to my final point of criticism regarding Žižek's reading of Kusturica, and that is the question of nationalism— more specifically of Žižek's implicit nationalism. Žižek tends to portray himself as an outsider, a dissident figure aligned to the new social movements and in opposition to nationalism and the Slovene state (Žižek & Salecl 1996). As I discussed in the previous chapter, in the first free elections of the newly independent state of Slovenia Žižek stood as a candidate for the "nationalist" Liberal Democratic Party, and as late as 1995 he was claiming that "our" party saved Slovenia (Parker 2004, pp. 34–5). His relationship with the new social movements was also rather ambiguous. As the former Yugoslavia started to unravel in a series of increasingly bloody conflicts, Žižek's political interventions in Slovenia increasingly focused on other people's pathologies (such as the "Western" gaze and Serbian nationalism), and never broached the dark side of Slovene politics or his own party's role in a deepening nationalism, xenophobia and curtailment of human rights (I will return to this in the next chapter).[7] Žižek was not alone in this and the new social movements were themselves caught in a peculiar, and politically regressive, dialectic. I will take two central issues here, anti-militarism and anti-authoritarianism, to illustrate the dynamic of this dialectic of nationalism and resistance. Both issues pitted the new social movements against the Belgrade government. The Yugoslav National Army (JNA) was increasingly identified with the Serbian Republic and Milošović's response to the rise in influence of the new social movements was calling for a "recentralization" of power. The new social movements, therefore, identified the main obstacle to reform and democratization as "outside" Slovenia in the form of Serbian nationalism and a specific state formation:

> Critique of a particular state form … cemented itself into a critique of Yugoslav society as inherently nationalist/Serbia and totalitarianist/Stalinist. The only liberation could, therefore, come from sovereignty and independence.
>
> *(Rizman 1995, quoted in Stubbs 1996, p. 8)*

By the time of the first free elections in the 1990s the question was not, as one sociologist of the new social movements puts it, whether or not the "soft nationalism" of the new social movements differed from other forms of nationalism, but how this soft nationalism had come to dominate the discourse of the new social movements and how opposition to militarism and authoritarianism had become identified with an emerging, independent, sovereign Slovene state (Stubbs 1996).

Let me return here to Žižek by way of the quotation above from his "Multiculturalism" article (Žižek 1997c). In this passage Žižek runs together the criticism of two films and two directors: Kusturica's *Underground* and Milcho Manchevski's *Before the Rain*. The two films become indistinguishable ideological products for the Western liberal gaze, but these films are very different stylistically, in terms of content and in terms of structure. While Kusturica has developed a frantic carnivalesque "aesthetic of chaos" (Halligan 2000), Manchevski's cinematography evokes a more mythical, timeless landscape, and the pace of his film is much slower and more contemplative. In relation to content, *Underground* depicts the course of history over a 50-year period. *Before the Rain*, however, does not address that history or the recent Balkan conflicts directly and is essentially a series of love stories. The narrative structure of the two films is also significantly different: *Underground* suggests a cyclical return of violence; *Before the Rain* does not. Indeed, *Before the Rain* does not have a circular narrative at all, but rather a Nietzschean "eternal return" which leaves open the possibility of historical change. So why does Žižek run together these two films, when he knows full well that the majority of his readership will not have seen either of them?

That is precisely the point, I think—that the majority of his readers would not know the films and therefore would be unable to distinguish between them.[8] The films simply become exemplary of a Western gaze projecting its phantasmatic content on an exotic "Slavic" other. Keith Brown (1998) has analyzed the reception of *Before the Rain* in terms of its domestic and international audiences, and this analysis has certain parallels with the reception of *Underground*, especially Žižek's polemic. In brief, while many European and North American critics eulogized over Manchevski's cinematography and other-worldly "fairytale" landscapes, these landscapes held deep historical resonance for a domestic audience. What was taken internationally to be a transnational hybrid production on universal themes and values was seen locally to be the production of a sovereign nation-state by a national director and anticipating the emergence of this nation on the international stage. The reception of *Before the Rain*, then, was split between a domestic and an international audience who appeared to be watching very different films. Something similar can be said for *Underground* and we need to distinguish the reception of this film between a domestic and an international audience.

From an international perspective the majority of the audience did not know where, for instance, Maribor was and who the crowds cheering the Nazis were.

For a domestic audience, however, this clearly was an issue. Žižek's equalizing of these two films can be seen as part of a wider discourse then taking place at the research institute in Ljubljana, where Žižek was based, and in Slovenia generally. According to Erik Tängerstad:

> [M]ost of the Slovenian critics view these films as naïve and simplifying, describing the conflict through ethnically and historically tainted stereotypes. However, when they were working out a Slovenian and/or Central European discourse around these two films, also a Slovenian intellectual and/or national identity could be said to have been in the making.
>
> *(Tängerstad 2000, pp. 175–181)*

By running these two films together Žižek is participating in the nascent nationalist rhetoric of Slovenia in the 1990s, which sought to distance and distinguish Slovenes from the southern Slavs of Serbia, Montenegro and Macedonia. This has been referred to by Balkan scholars as "nesting orientalism"—that is to say, the orientalizing of other ethnic identities within the Balkans themselves (Bakić-Hayden 1995). By blurring the distinction between Serbs and Macedonians in this case, Žižek is doing precisely what he is accusing others, in particular Western liberals and leftists, of doing—that is to say, seeing the other as an undifferentiated mass upon which we, now including Central Europeans, project our phantasmatic content and distinguish ourselves.

Žižek's reading and polemical deployment of recent Balkan films such as *Underground* and *Before the Rain* does not undermine his analysis of the fantasy structure of nationalist ideology or of the nation as *das Ding*. However, as with Kusturica's "choice" in rejecting Bosnian nationalism, Žižek's critique of Serb nationalism, however unwittingly, serves to endorse the dominant nationalist ideological rhetoric of Slovenia in the 1990s. We might see this in terms of what Michael Billig has called "banal nationalism"—the way in which national identity pervades everyday life. Nationalism is not necessarily something that is extreme or extrinsic to the daily lives of subjects but something that is continually "flagged" up through our everyday practices (Billig 1995). As the Althusserian literary critic Pierre Macherey (1978) used to argue, a text's ideology is apparent not through what it says but through what it does not say, its gaps and silences. Žižek's nationalism is evident not in his published texts and statements so much as through his preoccupation with the pathologies of others and his continuing silence in relation to Slovenia.

Notes

1 As the editors of the volume *Balkan as Metaphor* point out, the rejection of Kusturica's films is now *de rigueur* for many Balkan intellectuals and it may be time to resignify these films "as cultural sites of genuine resistance and triumphant critique, rather than as

an apology for nationalism" (Bjelić & Savić 2002, p. 15). This chapter is very much in the spirit of resignifying Kusturica's *Underground*, but I would not wish to defend any of his subsequent films, or indeed his subsequent extreme nationalist politics culminating in "Solidarity—Kosovo is Serbia" campaign.

2 Srđjan Dragojević's *Pretty Village, Pretty Flame*. This film was also greeted with accusations of Serb propaganda upon release.
3 See Homer (2009) for a fuller analysis of this film.
4 It is not clear that Hegel ever wrote this, and Marx seems to be developing the idea from his correspondence with Engels. Marx, of course, never believed that history repeated itself in this fashion.
5 *Underground*, for example, makes explicit reference to both Makavejev's *WR: Mysteries of the Organism* and Francis Ford Coppola's *Apocalypse Now*, which again suggests that Kusturica is locating his film within a tradition of anti-war cinematic production (see Iordanova (2002, Ch. 3) for a discussion of the intertextual references and "makeovers" in *Underground*).
6 As Kay notes, Žižek shares another affinity with Adorno and Marcuse in terms of his taste in art and culture generally, which is very much that of a European intellectual and not at all popular despite the introductions to Lacan through popular culture (Kay 2003, p. 71).
7 Personal correspondence with Slovene activists.
8 In the "Ethnic Cleansing" version of this article Žižek does distinguish the ethnicity of the directors, but he does not do so in the more widely circulated "Multiculturalism" version. It is also possible, following on from Žižek's comments in the documentary *Žižek!* (2005), that he does not watch the films that he discusses because this may spoil the theoretical point he wishes to make, that he has not seen either film, although I am not convinced that one should take these comments too seriously.

References

Bakić-Hayden, M. (1995) Nesting Orientalism: The Case of Former Yugoslavia. *Slavic Review* 54(4): 917–931.
Billig, M. (1995) *Banal Nationalism*. London: Sage Publications.
Bjelić, D.I. (2005) Global Aesthetics and Serbian Cinema in the 1990s. In Imre, A. (ed.) *East European Cinemas*. London: Routledge.
Bjelić, D.I. & Savić, O. (eds) (2002) *Balkan as Metaphor: Between Globalization and Fragmentation*. Cambridge, MA: MIT Press.
Brown, K. (1998) Macedonian Culture and its Audiences: An Analysis of Before the Rain. In Hughes-Freehand, F. (ed.) *Ritual, Performance, Media*. London: Routledge.
Gocić, G. (2001) *Notes from the Underground: The Cinema of Emir Kusturica*. London: Wallflower Press.
Halligan, B. (2000) An Aesthetic of Chaos. In Horton, A.J. (ed.) *The Celluloid Tinderbox: Yugoslav Screen Reflections of a Turbulent Decade*. Shropshire: Central Europe Review.
Homer, S. (2009) Retrieving Kusturica's *Underground* as a Critique of Ethnic Nationalism. *Jump Cut: A Review of Contemporary Media* 5(1). www.ejumpcut.org/archive/jc51.2009/index.html (accessed 30 November 2015).
Iordanova, D. (2001) *Cinema of Flames: Balkan Film, Culture and the Media*. London: BFI Publishing.
Iordanova, D. (2002) *Emir Kusturica*. London: BFI Publishing.
Kay, S. (2003) *Žižek: A Critical Introduction*. Cambridge: Polity Press.

Lacan, J. (2006 [1957]) Seminar on "The Purloined Letter". In Fink, B. (trans.) *Écrits*. New York: W.W. Norton & Co.

Longinović, T.Z. (2005) Playing the Western Eye: Balkan Masculinity and Post-Yugoslav War Cinema. In Imre, A. (ed.) *East European Cinemas*. London: Routledge.

Macherey, P. (1978) *A Theory of Literary Production*. London: Routledge and Kegan Paul.

Marx, K. (1973 [1969]) The Eighteenth Brumaire of Louis Bonaparte. In Fernbach, D. (ed.) *Surveys from Exile*. Harmondsworth: Penguin.

Parker, I. (2004) *Slavoj Žižek: A Critical Introduction*. London: Pluto Press.

Stubbs, P. (1996) Nationalism, Globalisation and Civil Society in Croatia and Slovenia. *Research in Social Movements, Conflicts and Change* 19: 1–26.

Tängerstad, E. (2000) Before the Rain—After the War? *Rethinking History* 4(2): 175–181.

Žižek, S. (1990) Eastern Europe's Republics of Gilead. *New Left Review* (I) 183. pp. 50–62.

Žižek, S. (1993) *Tarrying with the Negative: Kant, Hegel and the Critique of Ideology*. Durham, NC: Duke University Press.

Žižek, S. (1994) *The Metastases of Enjoyment: Six Essays on Woman and Causality*. London: Verso.

Žižek, S. (1997a) Underground, or Ethnic Cleansing as a Continuation of Poetry by Other Means. *InterCommunication* 18. www.ntticc.or.jp/pub/ic_mag/ic018/intercity/zizek_E.html (accessed 30 November 2015).

Žižek, S. (1997b) *The Plague of Fantasies*. London: Verso.

Žižek, S. (1997c) Multiculturalism, or, the Cultural Logic of Multinational Capitalism. *New Left Review* (I) 225. pp. 28–51.

Žižek, S. (2000) *The Fragile Absolute—or, Why is the Christian Legacy Worth Fighting For?* London: Verso.

Žižek, S. (2001) *On Belief*. London: Routledge.

Žižek, S. (2008) The Military-Poetic Complex. *London Review of Books* 30(16). p. 17.

Žižek, S. & Salecl, R. (1996) Lacan in Slovenia: Slavoj Žižek and Renata Salecl. Interview with Dews, P. & Osborne, P. In Osborne, P. (ed.) *A Critical Sense: Interviews with Intellectuals*. London: Routledge.

Filmography

Before the Rain/Pred dozhdot (1994) Film. Directed by Milcho Manchevski. [DVD] Macedonia/France/UK.

Pretty Village, Pretty Flame/Lepa sela, lepo gore (1996) Film. Directed by Srđjan Dragojević. [DVD] Yugoslavia.

Underground: Once Upon a Time There Was a Country/Podzemlje: Bila jednom jedna zemlja (1995) Film. Directed by Emir Kusturica. [DVD] France/Germany/Hungary.

Žižek! (2005) Film. Directed by Astra Taylor. [DVD] USA/Canada.

3

TO BEGIN AT THE BEGINNING AGAIN

Žižek in Yugoslavia

In *First as Tragedy, Then as Farce* (2009a), Žižek suggests that it is time to "start over again." He approvingly quotes Vladimir Lenin's remark that communists who have no illusions, and who preserve their strength and flexibility "to begin from the beginning" over and over again on approaching an extremely difficult task, will not perish. This is Lenin at his "Beckettian best," he continues: "Try again. Fail again. Fail better" (Žižek 2009a, p. 86). The lesson Žižek draws from Lenin, however, is not that we must make one more effort, one more push towards "true" socialism, but rather that we return to the starting point itself. *First as Tragedy* thus concludes with a resounding call to the international left to "not be afraid, join us, come back! You've had your anti-communist fun, and you are pardoned for it—time to get serious once again" (ibid., p. 157).

Žižek's call to get serious, learn from our mistakes, and start the "patient ideological-critical work" (Žižek 2009a, p. 7) of castrating those in power is heartening but surely the key question to ask is what it is we are being welcomed back to. Here Žižek endorses Alain Badiou's recent stance:

> The communist hypothesis remains the right hypothesis ... If this hypothesis should have to be abandoned, then it is not worth doing anything in the order of collective action. Without the perspective of communism, without this Idea, nothing in the historical and political future is of such a kind as to interest the philosopher. Each individual can pursue their private business and we won't mention it again.
>
> *(Badiou, quoted in Žižek 2009a, p. 87)*

For Badiou, we must retrieve the "Idea" of communism, which is not to say that we simply repeat the "obscure disaster" of twentieth-century communism but that we rethink the general framework itself from the ground up. This is not an entirely new idea for Žižek and, as he puts it in "Repeating Lenin" (2000), the idea itself is not to repeat the mistakes of the past but to repeat what Lenin "FAILED TO DO, his MISSED opportunities" (Žižek 2000, p. 20, emphasis in the original). If we are "seriously" to assess Žižek's recent political interventions, then we must take him at his word and return to the beginning to assess those interventions, what his missed opportunities were and what he failed to do.

This return calls for a return to Yugoslavia as the context of Žižek's intellectual beginning, a beginning habitually ignored or omitted by his Western commentators.[1] For example, Jodi Dean (2006a) locates the development of Žižek's politics and thought in relation to a formidable list of Western European—and one North American—thinkers but completely ignores his formative experience in the former Yugoslavia. This decontextualization facilitates Dean's next move which is to recontextualize him within "the problems and concerns presently occupying contemporary American political theorists" (Dean 2006a, p. xxi). Žižek thus provides the answer to the North American left's current impasse. Dean endorses Žižek's emphasis on the party as the provider of "the formal position of Truth," but ignores Žižek's relation to his own former party. Once we recognize the formal role of the party, Dean argues, we can then understand Žižek's answer to the question "What is to be done?" In a word: nothing (ibid., p. 197).

To do nothing, however, is not a recipe for inactivity but an injunction to "Bartleby politics"—that is to say, an act of "refusal as such" (Žižek 2006, p. 384) for which there is no determinate content. I will come back to this below. Similarly, Adrian Johnston (2009) adopts the position that "it isn't valid to evaluate the ideas of other philosophers in light of their behind-the-texts activities," especially when the "historically specific details of their non-textual interventions and socio-political situations are long forgotten by everyone save for a few specialist intellectual historians and biographers" (ibid., p. xxii). While I agree that Žižek's political interventions may not invalidate his philosophy, they do tell us something about his politics and, as Žižek frequently reminds us, he is not simply playing intellectual games; his intentions are "ruthlessly radical," and he is serious about changing the world. In this sense his actual interventions matter (Žižek 2003, p. 503). Given the complexity of Žižek's politics, it behooves us to scrutinize his praxis in order to understand better how this highly seductive theory plays out in practice.

There is chaos in the universe

Žižek has recently taken to lambasting armchair radicals with the sayings of Mao Zedong, in particular the quote "there is great disorder under heaven, the situation is excellent" (Žižek 2010a, p. xii). Academic leftists, he argues, have been waiting for the system to collapse and hoping for a revolution for so long that they should be pleased it is now actually taking place. Žižek is right. The left has for decades wished for a systemic crisis that would bring about radical social transformation, and now that the crisis is here they should be seizing the moment. This is not the position that he adopted when the crisis hit the former Yugoslavia, however. Once in power, the Slovene Liberal Democratic Party was the party of capital (Parker 2004, pp. 33–4), and Žižek's response in subsequent interviews when asked about the policies of the Liberals in government was that the party saved the country from chaos (Žižek 1996b). He even went so far as to suggest that if a little neo-liberal privatization of the economy worked then, why not try it (Žižek 1996a, p. 32). Žižek took the side of the state against the social movements and he is quite clear he would do so again today: "I should say that in the break-up of Yugoslavia just as in most other conflicts between the state and civil society, I was regularly on the side of the state. Civil society meant democratic opposition; it also meant, however, violent nationalism" (Badiou & Žižek 2009, p. 65).

There are a number of problems with taking this last assertion at face value. First, as previously noted (Chapter 1), in an interview with *Radical Philosophy* Žižek characterized the position of the new Liberal Democratic Party rather differently, namely as part of the democratic opposition closely aligned with the new social movements, especially feminism and environmentalism. With their ideology of pluralism, ecological preservation and protection of minority rights, the Liberals saw themselves very much in the tradition of radical democratic liberalism. What was distinctive about their position, argued Žižek, was their opposition to populist nationalism (Žižek & Salecl 1996, p. 28). The second issue turns on the false choice we are being presented between the state on the one hand and a democratic but nationalist opposition on the other. Without any context in which to assess these alternatives, the choice seems quite straightforward, with everyone opposed to nationalism opting for the state. What this false dichotomy leaves out, however, are the presence of non-nationalist opposition movements in Yugoslavia (Gordy 1999) and an acknowledgment that the Slovene state, including the Liberals once in power, was also nationalist (Woodward 1995, Ch. 3). More often than not, the only context we have for understanding Žižek's interventions is the one he provides, which is often problematic.

Defending the legacy of European Enlightenment

Though Žižek has certainly been radicalized over the past two decades, he continues to return to previous interventions, which now sit rather uneasily with his current political positions. His views on European anti-immigration policies and the Roma, for example, remain split between those applied outside Slovenia and those operating within. In *First as Tragedy* Žižek argues that the only principled political stance we can adopt today against the European Union's (EU) racist immigration policies is to endorse the slogan of Badiou's *L'Organisation Politique*:

"those who are here are from here." This is a fine principle and one that, as Žižek says, "has a direct link to reality" (Žižek 2009a, pp. 118–19). It is a principle he restated in his support for 287 migrant workers on hunger strike in Athens and Thessaloniki, Greece, in the spring of 2011. Žižek offered the hunger strikers his full solidarity, arguing that they were fighting for more than just their rights; they were fighting for the future of Europe and its legacy of universal emancipation.[2]

I fully endorse Žižek's (2010b) views here and agree that the fight against the "reasonable racism" of European politicians, such as British Prime Minister David Cameron, former French President Nicolas Sarkozy and German Chancellor Angela Merkel, will be one of the defining moments for the future of the EU. This is a rather different principle, however, from the one applied in Slovenia in 1992, when approximately 20,000 migrant workers were erased from the register of permanent residents and immediately became illegal immigrants (Bjelić 2009, pp. 503–7). I am not suggesting that Žižek was involved in the decision to erase these people, but, as a part of DEMOS, the Slovene Democratic Opposition, he was a prominent member of the Liberal Democratic Party which was then in government and passed these anti-immigrant laws. Along with many other prominent members of DEMOS, Žižek remained silent on the issue—he did "nothing"—and in subsequent interviews he has defended these actions against his critics (Žižek 1996b).[3] If this is not simply a case of NIMBY (not in my back yard) politics then what is it? What happened to the Liberal Democratic Party's defense of minority rights, and why should we support the rights of immigrants as a universal principle except in the case of Slovenia? Indeed, his silence on the issue of the erased is in marked contrast to the position of radicals within Slovenia today.[4]

It may seem unreasonable to condemn Žižek for views he expressed over 20 years ago, as today he argues that immigrants should not be satisfied with the "normalizing" strategies of the EU: "It is not enough to find new terms with which to define oneself outside of the dominant … tradition," writes Žižek; "one should go a step further and deprive the [majority] of the monopoly on defining their own tradition" (Žižek 2009a, p. 120). In short, we should reject the sham tolerance of multiculturalism, which accepts the other only insofar as the other is detoxified and does not disturb our comfortable liberal world or intrude on our space (Žižek 2010b). Immigrants should forcefully and unapologetically assert their rights. In doing so, they are defending nothing less than the European legacy of emancipation.[5] Immigrants are an issue of consideration once more in Žižek's *Living in the End Times*, although here they are Roma in Slovenia:

> [I]n Slovenia recently, a big problem arose with a Roma family who were camping close to a small town. When a man was killed in the camp, the townspeople started to protest, demanding that the Roma be moved from the camp (which they had occupied illegally) to another location, organizing vigilante groups etc. Predictably, Slovenian liberals condemned them as racists, locating racism in this isolated small town, though the liberals, living

comfortably in the big cities, had no contact with the Roma other than meeting their representatives in front of the TV cameras. When the TV reporters interviewed the "racists" from the town, it became clear they were a group of people frightened by the constant fighting and shooting in the Roma camp, by the theft of animals from their farms, and by other forms of minor harassment. It is all too easy to say (as did the liberals) that the Roma way of life is (also) a consequence of centuries of exclusion and mistreatment, that the townspeople should be more receptive to the Roma, and so on and so forth. What nobody was prepared to do vis-à-vis the local "racists" was offer concrete solutions for the very real problems the Roma camp evidently posed for them.

(Žižek 2010a, pp. 45–6)

This extraordinary, and appalling, paragraph could have been written by Sarkozy himself, as he expelled the Roma from France for "illegally" setting up camps, engaging in criminal activities, and terrorizing local populations with violence.[6] I take Žižek to be referring to an incident concerning the Strojan family who lived in the village of Ambrus. In November 2006 a mob of villagers attacked approximately 30 members of the family after one of them was involved in a criminal incident. The minister of the interior persuaded the family to leave the village temporarily and then told the mob that the family would never return. The family was resettled in an isolated area owned by the Ministry of Defense, their homes were destroyed, and over a year later they remained without a proper residence. It would seem that defending a principle in France or Greece while living comfortably in London is one thing, but applying the same principle to one's own country is another (Zorn 2009, p. 218).[7] Suddenly, it seems, we must show understanding to racists and offer "concrete solutions" to a "very real problem." Whatever happened to fighting for the emancipatory legacy of the European Enlightenment, one might ask? Indeed, what has happened to the distinction between a radical politics of the act, which reconfigures the entire socio-symbolic field and mere political activity, which serves to shore-up the existing political order? This distinction, as we will see below, appears to be rather arbitrarily applied. It would appear that fidelity to the truth of the party and the passive refusal to take a stance can both support the symbolic order of late capitalism and undermine it equally as well. There seems to be nothing particularly radical in do-nothing politics. This is not, however, what Žižek means by either the party or acts of radical refusal.

The politics of not-all

The party can only be presented to us as the solution to our present impasse, insofar as the party as such does not exist, but rather it is a purely formal designation that can never be immanently present. Rex Butler (2005) clearly elucidates how such a procedure takes place, arguing that Žižek's politics are a politics of the party but that this is not the party as we knew it:

The Party *formalizes* the Revolution in the sense that it institutionalizes it, gives it structure, breaks with the ideology of "spontaneism" and "popular sentiment" … But at the same time as this "immanence," there is also something else to be seen. It is to think that, despite the emphasis on the actual practice of Lenin, his institutionalization of Marx, there is nevertheless a certain "Lenin" beyond any such "Leninism," or a Lenin "beyond" Stalin. That is, if the destiny of Marxism is to be institutionalized, it is also to be what would render this forever incomplete.

(Butler 2005, pp. 118–19)

Žižek's language of the party is "precise" but we do not have to worry about the actualization of the party insofar as it can never be immanently present. We repeat something only insofar as it is unfinished and has yet to happen. Moreover, it can never happen in the sense of a full self-presence, as repetition is governed by the feminine logic of the not-all.

For Butler, repetition and incompletion (Lacan's not-whole) are the keys to understanding Žižek's politics. Briefly stated, in psychoanalysis repetition is associated with the death drive and the idea of repetition compulsion. Lacan extended the notion of repetition, deeming it the general characteristic of the symbolic order itself, insofar as the signifying chain operates through repetition. From a psychoanalytic perspective we are doomed to repeat and it is through this repetition that something comes from nothing. Repetition, as Butler writes, "only repeats what is already therefore before … and reveals that what is does not exist before this repetition" (Butler 2005, p. 26). Repetition is the recurrence of a certain experience of impossibility and gives rise to what Butler defines as a politics of the not-all (ibid., p. 132). The woman, for Lacan, is defined as that which is not wholly within the symbolic order and thus experiences a form of *jouissance* beyond the symbolic law of castration (Lacan 1998, pp. 71–77). Unlike the masculine logic of exception, the feminine logic of not-all suggests that the process itself becomes its own self-exception, in the sense that there is no exception to this process and yet we cannot say exactly what the process actually is because it is its own exception. This is precisely how concepts such as "party" or "class" work for Žižek. Class is not an exception, in the sense that it is excluded from the social as that which the social cannot accommodate or tolerate, but it is that which renders the social "not-all." There is no social without class, and class is precisely that which cannot be accounted for within the social. This is one definition of the Lacanian Real.

For Butler, Žižek's politics are entirely formal, as he does not offer a coherent political or ethical program, and his interventions are specifically historical and contextually determined. Indeed, all Žižek tells us is the form that such interventions must take. Thus Marxism, like psychoanalysis, is a formalism and, in this sense, offers no coherent world view, identifiable program or procedure.

Many Marxists today would take issue with this view. Fredric Jameson, for one, has long argued that Marxism reduced to a mere method of historical analysis, which does not project an alternative future or alternate set of social relations, is worse than dead—it is utterly worthless (Jameson 1983, p. 297). Such projections are the function of ideology rather than science and Jameson has consistently advocated developing a properly Marxist ideology to accompany its scientific and historical method. In *Archaeologies of the Future* (2005) Jameson demonstrates this very point in his controversial discussion of the transitional demand for full employment as a utopian fantasy that is at once "practical and revolutionary," in the sense that the demand "could not be realized without transforming the system beyond recognition" (Jameson 2005, p. 147).

Terry Eagleton argues that Marxism is a specific unity of theory and practice, of utopian vision and hard-nosed realism, and that if we as socialists are to break with the present state of things then we must be "prepared to spell out in some detail how this would be achieved, and what institutions it would involve" (Eagleton 2011, p. 73). This does not mean that we can foresee the future or that there is any kind of teleology involved here, but it does suggest that we need to think about what kind of society we want and how we might get there.

Similarly, Erik Olin Wright's (2010) project on envisioning real utopias sets out to identify existing institutional practices that prefigure radical alternatives to capitalism. Jameson, Eagleton and Wright not only offer us a trenchant critique of capital, as Žižek does, but also put forward specific proposals to debate and struggle for. For Žižek, though, the proper political act is just to keep open a fundamental choice; there is no content to this choice, just the form of maintaining it. In short, Žižek "fundamentally *has nothing to say*" (Butler 2005, pp. 122–23, emphasis in the original). It is this politics of the not-all that allows Žižek's supporters easily to accommodate all his talk of class struggle, revolution and the party without worrying too much about the implications of these things in actuality. They become empty signifiers (in Laclau's sense) that each of us can invest with whatever form of politics suits us. It is telling that when Žižek does make specific political statements—such as his politically incorrect remarks on the 2005 Paris riots or the necessity of organizing and politicizing the slum dwellers of Latin America—his commentators immediately take offence (Žižek 2005; Dean 2005; Butler & Stephens 2006; Dean 2006b). I agree with Butler that Žižek's interventions are historically specific and contextually determined, but does this not oblige us to scrutinize that context in order to determine how this formal choice positions him?

Taking sides

Butler argues that what is radical about Žižek's position is precisely his refusal to take sides and his insistence on maintaining a position of undecidability in politics—that is to say, to refuse to accept the terms of the false choice we are offered. Here he cites the 1999 North Atlantic Treaty Organization (NATO) bombing of Serbia and Žižek's position against the double blackmail of refusing NATO and supporting Milošević, or refusing Milošević and supporting NATO (Žižek 1999). Both sides of this forced choice are equally bad, and thus the only radical thing to do is refuse the choice itself and keep open the formal possibility of a real one. So far so good, but there are two problems with this position. First, Žižek is quite clear in his recent books that the only principled position we can take today is to take sides (Žižek 2009a, p. 6), whether for or against global capital (Žižek 2009b, p. 421). Second, he has always taken sides and originally took a position on the NATO bombing that was pro-NATO, and subsequently erased this position in his later publications (see Chapter 1). By contrast, many on the Western European left and within the former Yugoslavia tried to maintain the difficult position of supporting neither the NATO bombing nor Milošević's nationalism. The problem once again is that Žižek supplies the context, which is then uncritically accepted by his advocates.

Žižek's analysis of the rise of so called Islamo-fascism in Afghanistan and Europe provides another intriguing example of this dynamic. He observes that only 30 years ago countries such as Afghanistan and Bosnia had strong secular traditions, which raises the question of what happened to these traditions. "Back in the 1970s and 1980s," Bosnia and Herzegovina "was (multi)culturally the most interesting and lively of all the Yugoslav republics, with an internationally recognized cinema school and a unique style of rock music." How then do we account for the rise of fundamentalism in Bosnia? "The root cause of this regression," writes Žižek, "lies in the desperate situation of Bosnian Muslims during the 1992–95 war, when they were basically abandoned by the Western powers to the Serb guns" (Žižek 2009a, pp. 73–74). What is interesting about these recent references to Sarajevo and the siege of this vibrant, multicultural center of creativity is how profoundly Western European they are. The Balkan film scholar Dina Iordanova (2001) has observed that Sarajevo was something of a cultural backwater during the 1970s and 1980s in relation to the other republics.[8] Indeed this was part of the distinctiveness of Emir Kusturica's early films.[9] The idea of Sarajevo as a multicultural, cosmopolitan city—and since when, one might ask, has Žižek been so interested in multiculturalism?—is largely a construct of the Western European media, one that Žižek is now reproducing.[10]

The issue of Western Europe's response to the plight of Bosnian Muslims is complex and I cannot possibly address the subject adequately here. It does serve to raise the problematic issue of taking Žižek at his word on Yugoslavia, however. He takes Toni Negri to task in a footnote to *In Defense of Lost Causes*:

> Another of Negri's weirdly inadequate readings is his note on the post-Yugoslav war, where he fully endorses the disintegration of Yugoslavia as the result of a dark plot by Germany, Austria, and the Vatican, which sustained financially and ideologically murderous nationalisms; plus, as expected, he insists on the equally distributed guilt … The inadequacy of this reading, as well as its pro-Serb bias, cannot but strike the eye: if the agents of the

disintegration of Yugoslavia were the separatist Croats and Slovenes, then the Serbs are *less* guilty … Plus it is not clear how to account in these terms for the original moment of the crisis, the Kosovan problem and the rise to power of Milošević.

(Žižek 2009b, p. 510, note 54)

Is this really such a weird and inadequate reading of the situation? In *Balkan Tragedy*, her authoritative study of the break-up of Yugoslavia, Susan Woodward notes that from the mid-1980s Austria and the Vatican "had pursued a strategy to increase their sphere of economic and spiritual influence in central and Eastern Europe, respectively" (Woodward 1995, pp. 148–149). Slovenia began economic collaboration with Austria as early as 1988 (ibid., p. 97), and they began secretly buying arms from the West in 1990 (ibid., p. 137). At the same time, Croatia was illegally buying arms from Hungary (ibid., p. 149). This was the same year that meetings were held between Milošević and Franco Tuđjman to divide Yugoslavia between Serbia and Croatia, with Serbia getting Kosovo in return for Croatia taking control of the Krajina (ibid., p. 139; Gowan 1999). From 1987 onwards, argues Woodward, the leaders "in Slovenia and Serbia were pursuing the same goal: putting what they defined as the national interests of their republics and nations above those of Yugoslavia" (Woodward 1995, p. 93). What differed were not their positions as such but their styles. To argue that nationalist forces in Croatia and Slovenia also played a significant role in the violent break-up of Yugoslavia is not to absolve the Serbian leadership of guilt but it is to refuse the false logic by which the West demonizes one side of the conflict while exempting itself and its allies in the former Yugoslavia of any responsibility for the violence that took place. If we are to avoid repeating the mistakes of the past, it would also be good to know how Slovenia's secession from Yugoslavia helped the Kosovars (or the Bosniaks, for that matter).[11]

Žižek's enthusiasm for Bosnian multiculturalism has also manifested itself recently in the celebration of Sarajevo's *New Primitivs* as exemplars of traversing the fantasy or over-identification:

> Instead of bemoaning the tragic fate of the Bosnians, [*The Top List of the Surrealists*] daringly mobilized all the clichés about the "stupid Bosnians" which were a commonplace in Yugoslavia, fully identifying with them—the point thus made was that the path of true solidarity leads through direct confrontation with the obscene racist fantasies which circulated in the symbolic space of Bosnia, through playful identification with them, not through the denial of these obscenities in the name of "what people are really like."
>
> *(Žižek 2009b, pp. 329–30)*[12]

After breaking with the *Neue Slowenische Kunst* (NSK) when they began to insist, in the mid-1990s, that their role in the national revival in Slovenia had not been properly recognized (Žižek 2007, p. 232), Žižek started to use the *New Primitivs* as a replacement for *Laibach* and the NSK as an exemplar of subversive cultural politics. What I am not clear about is how this newfound example of cultural politics sits with Žižek's critique of Kusturica as the poet of ethnic cleansing (see Chapter 2), given that Kusturica was closely associated with the *New Primitivs*. Kusturica fell out with his former associates in Sarajevo over the issue of nationalism and "The No Smoking Orchestra" split, with one group remaining in Sarajevo during the siege and another based in Belgrade. Kusturica was with the latter (Levi 2007, p. 62). Again, Žižek's references to the vibrant and subversive multicultural life of Sarajevo only work if his commentators never get past his own contextualization and are not interested in the opposition movements that challenged both Milošević and other nationalist movements in the former Yugoslavia (Gordy 1999; Lazić 1999).

The Leninist gesture

Žižek's Leninist turn in the early 2000s marks a break with his previous post-Marxist interlocutors and an explicit radicalization of his work. The 2001 conference "The Retrieval of Lenin" in Essen, Germany, was attended by nearly every major academic Marxist writing today, as well as leading activists of the Trotskyite left, and Žižek's new post-Maoist friends. The conference was also contemporaneous with the publication of Žižek's dialogue with Judith Butler and Ernesto Laclau, *Contingency, Hegemony, Universality* (2000).[13] What started as a dialogue "to establish the common trajectory of [their] thought and to stage in a productive way the different intellectual commitments" (Butler et al. 2000, p. 1) that they shared, eventually degenerated into an increasingly acrimonious exchange between Laclau and Žižek. In his final contribution to the volume, Laclau expresses his exasperation. He can discuss politics with Butler, because she talks about the real world and the strategic problems people face in their actual struggles, but with Žižek it is hopeless: "The only thing one gets from him are injunctions to overthrow capitalism or to abolish liberal democracy, which have no meaning at all" (ibid., p. 290). In the unlikely event, he continued, that Žižek's ideas were ever accepted, they would set the left back 50 years.

Ironically, what was crucial to the demarxification of Slovene politics was the introduction of Laclau and Mouffe's *Hegemony and Socialist Strategy* (1985) into the former Yugoslavia in the mid-1980s, through the journal *Mladina* and their association with Žižek (Pupovac 2006, p. 118). Žižek was at the time a member of the Committee for the Defense of Human Rights, a committee in defense of Janez Janša, a *Mladina* journalist and peace activist who later became the minister of defense and subsequently a right-wing prime minister and extreme nationalist. Žižek enthusiastically supported the committee's role in creating an open, pluralistic and "democratic front" as well as a renewed public sphere (or, "public space of democracy") (ibid., p. 129). As Ozren Pupovac notes, the committee

confirmed the political force of *Hegemony and Socialist Strategy*'s conceptual categories, and the work played a decisive role in the emergence of a "proper post-
socialist political sequence" in Slovenia (ibid., p. 130). Paradoxically, Žižek's
retrieval of Lenin sought to reverse a political situation that his own interventions
had played a significant role in creating.

Žižek concedes that the idea of "reactualizing" Lenin will today be greeted with
derision. Lenin stands for the failure to put Marxism into practice. He is a figure
of the past whose ideas—the party, revolution, and the dictatorship of the proletariat—
now seem outdated. However, to repeat Lenin is not to return to Lenin. Rather:

> to REPEAT Lenin does NOT mean a RETURN to Lenin—to repeat
> Lenin is to accept that "Lenin is dead," that his particular solution failed,
> even failed monstrously, but that there was a utopian spark in it worth
> saving. To repeat Lenin means that one has to distinguish between what
> Lenin effectively did and the field of possibilities that he opened up, the
> tension in Lenin between what he effectively did and another dimension,
> what was "in Lenin more than Lenin himself"
>
> *(Žižek 2000, p. 20, emphasis in the original)*

Žižek's Lenin is primarily the Lenin of *The State and Revolution* and other writings
from 1917 (Žižek 2002). That is to say, it is the Lenin who faced defeat (the
collapse of the Second International following the catastrophe of 1914), but
rather than succumb to resignation and the idea of a gradualist, reformist move
toward a socialist state, he reasserted the need for a violent revolution to
abolish the state.[14] The Leninist event—this break with the evolutionary historicism of the Second International—emerges from the recognition of "the
Truth of THIS catastrophe" (Žižek 2000, p. 9, emphasis in the original). Out of this
moment of despair arises the kernel of the Leninist "utopia," "the radical imperative
to smash the bourgeois state, which means the state AS SUCH, and to invent a new
communal social form without a standing army, police or bureaucracy, in which
all could take part in the administration of ... social matters" (ibid., p. 10).

The Leninist utopia arises, then, from the recognition of utter failure and the
demand for the impossible, for a complete social revolution, at a time when not
even the Bolshevik Party thought it possible. For Žižek, Lenin's greatness resides in
the fact that he was not afraid to succeed. He squarely faced the truth of the situation
and dared to think beyond the horizon of that failure. Lenin, writes Žižek,
"stands for the compelling FREEDOM to suspend the stale existing (post)ideological
coordinates, the debilitating [situation] in which we live—it simply means that
we are allowed to think again" (Žižek 2000, p. 10, emphasis in the original).

We should note here that Lenin's utopian spark is predicated upon an initial
act of negation, what Žižek calls "wiping the slate clean"—that is, smashing the
old state to allow the new to emerge. For Lenin, the state could not simply be
abolished overnight (this was the utopian dream of the anarchists); the proletariat

first had to win state power, and only then could it be smashed. The proletariat needs state power, writes Lenin, "a centralized organization of force, an organization of violence, both to crush the resistance of the exploiters and to lead the enormous mass of the population" in the task of constructing a socialist economy (Lenin 1968 [1917], p. 279). In contrast to many on the left today—such as Simon Critchley's strategy of making impossible demands upon the state (Žižek 2009b, p. 346), or Badiou's strategy of subtraction, of maintaining a distance from the state (see Chapter 4)—Žižek does not shy away from Lenin's insistence on the necessity of revolutionary violence and seizing control of the state.

There is an ambiguity running through Žižek's return to Lenin, however, which turns on the actuality of Lenin and his formalization. Žižek's return is a return to a politics of truth in the face of postmodern relativism and skepticism: "Lenin's wager—today, in our era of postmodern relativism, more actual than ever—is that truth and partisanship, the gesture of taking sides, are not only not mutually exclusive but condition each other: the *universal* truth in a concrete situation can only be articulated from a thoroughly *partisan* position. Truth is by definition one-sided" (Žižek 2000, p. 4). It is this partisan Lenin that Žižek wishes to reanimate—his mode of analysis, his discipline and above all his capacity to seize the moment, to intervene in the specific conjuncture.

As Evan Calder Williams has pointed out, though, the nature of this intervention remains problematic. There were at least two versions of Lenin being retrieved in Essen: the post-Maoist Lenin of Badiou and Žižek, with an emphasis on partisanship (notwithstanding their major differences) (Johnston 2009, pp. 133–34), and the Trotskyite Lenin of the party (Williams 2011, p. 159). While the notion of the party was frequently invoked, not least by Žižek himself, its actual form remained opaque and the question of how we might reanimate the notion of the party today was never directly addressed.

Writing from Greece, a country where the party retains the formal position of truth to such an extent that the different leftist parties will not march in the same demonstration as each other and in which this truth, for the communist party specifically, is unapologetically Stalinist, I find this more than a little problematic. Surely five decades of New Left and feminist critique of precisely this kind of party organization has taught us something, and to find the notion of the party simply invoked today without any consideration of its actualization seems perverse at best (I will return to the politics of the party in the next chapter). Paraphrasing Lenin's slogan, "advanced politics needs advanced theory," Williams observes that this particular retrieval of Lenin "remains a *theoretical* enterprise" (Williams 2011, p. 162), leaving aside the difficult issue of the party's form and organization. Žižek's Lenin, far from retrieving a Lenin beyond Lenin, appears to offer us a Leninism without Lenin.

Žižek has defended his pragmatism in response to the kinds of criticism that I have advanced above—namely, that his politics are inconsistent: "One of the standard reproaches to my political writings is that, when it comes to my

proposals of how to act, what is to be done, I oscillate between three options: (1) the 'Bartleby politics' of doing nothing; (2) preparing (or, rather, waiting) for a big violent radical Act, a total revolutionary upheaval; (3) engaging in local pragmatic interventions" (Žižek 2010c, p. 101; Žižek 2010a, p. 398). Žižek's answer is "guilty as charged," but then he asks why we have to choose in the first place. Different situations call for different kinds of politics, and in these "obscure times" in which we live, only a Leninist "concrete analysis of concrete circumstances" can show us the proper way to act (Žižek 2010c, p. 101).

I agree, but such an analysis is not present in Žižek's own work, and so the only way we have of assessing his politics is by looking at his specific interventions. The question also arises as to how such pragmatism is different from the kinds of postmodern politics Žižek attacks. One of the great attractions of Žižek's work in these relativistic times has been, for some of us at least, his universalist assertion of a politics of truth. As I have argued above, however, these principles seem to be applied rather arbitrarily. Lenin's formalization of Marx was forged in direct response to and in tension with the demands of a mass movement and the ebb and flow of class struggle. While there is plenty of resistance and struggle today, it is the mass movement that we are lacking—a movement that can endow our acts of resistance with enough consistency to challenge the system itself. Žižek does not have an answer to this dilemma any more than the rest of us and, as he constantly reminds us, if we are waiting for a philosopher to come up with the answer, we have already lost the cause. Unless his political categories—the party, class struggle, and revolutionary violence—are merely empty signifiers that theoretically formalize a process but do not commit one to any particular political position, then it is surely worth scrutinizing how these categories have been deployed in practice and whether they help us in answering questions of organization and strategy today. Žižek's ambiguous role in the politics of the former Yugoslav state provides us with an indication of how his theoretical interventions have played out in the past. We ignore them at our own cost.

Notes

1 Parker (2004) is the exception here.
2 After 44 days and with 100 of the hunger strikers hospitalized, the strike was called off on 9 March 2011. The "Socialist" government of Greece had authorized state-employed doctors to force feed anyone in imminent danger of death and reached a compromise granting the strikers' temporary residence.
3 It was this refusal to take a stance on the issue of the "erased" that created the rift between Žižek and the anti-capitalist and anti-racist movements in Slovenia at that time, and not simply personal animosity or jealousy, as Žižek implies in interviews.
4 In Slovenia the issue of the erased is also still very much alive. See Zorn & Čebron (2008); Kogovšek et al. (2010).
5 Žižek's response to the refugee crisis that has engulfed and divided the European Union since the summer of 2015 could not be more different; gone is the rhetoric of immigrants demanding their rights and thus defending the European legacy of

emancipation and in its place he provides a staunch defense of "our way of life." Žižek outlines four proposals to break the deadlock over the refugees: first, "Europe must reassert its commitment to provide for the dignified treatment of refugees" (2015a np). Second, "Europe should impose clear rules and regulations," including control over the movement of refugees and settlement in countries of the EUs choice; "no tolerance of religious, sexist or ethnic violence" and respect for individual freedom. Third, "a new kind of military and economic intervention will have to be invented – a kind of intervention that avoids the neocolonial traps of the recent past" (2015a np). Finally, "there is a need for radical economic change which would abolish the conditions that create refugees" (2015a np). Whilst it is easy for anyone on the left to agree with the first and last of these proposals, the second and third beg more questions than they answer. Who will decide which rules and regulations to impose and how will they be enforced? Will religious tolerance and respect for individual freedoms be enforced within the EU itself, on countries such as Hungary or Slovakia, as well as newly arriving refugees? What form might a non-colonial military intervention take? Was this not called "humanitarian intervention" in the 1990s? It is not clear what "legacy" is being defended here, it is certainly not emancipatory, and once again it seems that Žižek has chosen the side of those in power against the weak, the displaced and the disenfranchised. In a subsequent article published after the Paris attacks of 13 November 2015 Žižek defends his proposals and insists that we must break "leftist taboos" and accept the "fact that most of the refugees come from a culture that is incompatible with Western European notions of human rights" (2015b np). Leaving aside Žižek's repeated attacks on the discourse of human rights he concludes:

> Emacipatory politics should not be bound a priori by formal-democratic procedures of legitimization. No, people quite often do NOT know what they want, or do not want what they know, or they simply want the wrong thing.
>
> *(2015b np, emphasis in the original)*

So much for trust in the people.

6 Sarkozy's expulsion of Roma from France was prompted by an incident on 16 July 2010, when a Roma man drove through a police checkpoint in Saint Aignan, Loire. He knocked down a police officer and, as he drove through a subsequent checkpoint, he was shot. The following day approximately 50 Roma rioted, destroying a police station and attacking other government buildings. Sarkozy also justified his action on the basis that the Roma were illegally in France.

7 Let me be clear, I agree with the principle Žižek is advocating ("those who are here are from here"). I simply believe that that principle should be universally applied and, as Zorn (2009) argues, since Slovenia's emergence as a sovereign state in 1991, it has developed discriminatory immigration policies targeting people from the former Yugoslavia, especially the erased and the Roma (ibid., p. 211). I would like to thank Nikolai Jeffs for alerting me to the details of this incident.

8 Iordanova describes her brief passage through Sarajevo in the mid-1980s, where she found "an ordinary Balkan city, like any other in the region," with the prevailing media image at the time as a "deeply provincial, sleepy oriental town." It was the long siege of the city that replaced this with "the image of a dynamic cosmopolitan location that had now fallen pray [sic] to dark forces" (Iordanova 2001, p. 235).

9 In an interview in 2001 Kusturica described Sarajevo as a provincial backwater, where "sad, drunken railway men and taxi drivers" met in pubs and drank. Iordanova continues: "It was this provincialism and the traditionalism of the patriarchal and yet cozy isolation of Bosnia that Kusturica's early films reflected" (Iordanova 2002, pp. 50–60).

10 We must distinguish between a multi-ethnic city, which Sarajevo surely was, and a multicultural city in the sense that Žižek is discussing it here.

11 After a strike by Kosovan miners in 1989 Belgrade imposed a state of emergency on Kosovo. The Slovenes responded with the Ljubljana Declaration (1 March 1989), calling for greater democracy and the recognition of minority rights. The declaration was rejected by Belgrade and in 1990 Slovenia held the first "free" democratic elections, and withdrew from Yugoslavia later that year. Žižek is right that the issue of Kosovo and minority rights was central to the break-up of Yugoslavia, but I fail to see how Slovenia's secession from the Federal Republic was at all beneficial for those same minorities (see Magaš 1989, 1993, Ch. 1).
12 The *New Primitivs* spelt their name without the "e." For an account of the *New Primitivs*, see Levi (2007). *The Top List of the Surrealists* was originally a radio program and then a television show, and not, as Žižek suggests, a rock group (Žižek 2009b, p. 329).
13 The papers from the Essen conference were subsequently published as Budgen et al. 2007.
14 Insofar as the state, wrote Lenin, is an "organ of class *rule*, an organ for the *oppression* of one class by another" (Lenin 1968 [1917], p. 266), the proletariat cannot take over the existing state and use it for its own ends, it cannot be ameliorated. The bourgeois state is a manifestation of the irreconcilability of class antagonism and therefore it must be completely *smashed*, and this cannot take place without a violent revolution (ibid., p. 277).

References

Badiou, A. & Žižek, S. (2009) *Philosophy in the Present*. Ed. Engelmann, P., trans. Thomas, P. & Toscano, A. Cambridge: Polity Press.

Bjelić, D.I. (2009) Immigrants as the Enemy: Psychoanalysis and the Balkans' Self-Orientalism. *Slavonic and East European Review* 87(3): pp. 487–517.

Budgen, S., Kouvelakis, S. & Žižek, S. (eds) (2007) *Lenin Reloaded: Towards a Politics of Truth*. Durham, NC: Duke University Press.

Butler, J., Laclau, E. & Žižek, S. (2000) *Contingency, Hegemony, Universality: Contemporary Dialogues on the Left*. London: Verso.

Butler, R. (2005) *Slavoj Žižek: Live Theory*. London: Continuum.

Butler, R. & Stephens, S. (2006) Play Fuckin Loud: Žižek Versus the Left. *The Symptom* 7. www.lacan.com/newspaper7.htm (accessed 4 June 2010).

Dean, J. (2005) A Limit Experience: On Žižek's Recent Remarks. jdeanicite.typepad.com/i_cite/2005/11/a_limit_experie.html (accessed 4 June 2010).

Dean, J. (2006a) *Žižek's Politics*. London: Routledge.

Dean, J. (2006b) Žižek Versus Who? jdeanicite.typepad.com/i_cite/2006/04/zizek_versus_wh.html (accessed 4 June 2010).

Eagleton, T. (2011) *Why Marx was Right*. New Haven, CT: Yale University Press.

Gordy, E. (1999) *The Culture of Power in Serbia: Nationalism and the Destruction of Alternatives*. University Park: Pennsylvania State University Press.

Gowan, P. (1999) The NATO Powers and the Balkan Tragedy. *New Left Review* (I) 234. pp. 83–105.

Iordanova, D. (2001) *Cinema of Flames: Balkan Film, Culture and the Media*. London: BFI Publishing.

Iordanova, D. (2002) *Emir Kusturica*. London: BFI Publishing.

Jameson, F. (1983) Science versus Ideology. *Humanities in Society* 6.

Jameson, F. (2005) *Archaeologies of the Future: The Desire Called Utopia and Other Science Fictions*. London: Verso.

Johnston, A. (2009) *Badiou, Žižek and Political Transformations: The Cadence of Change*. Evanston, IL: Northwestern University Press.

Kogovšek, N. et al. (2010) *The Scars of the Erasure: A Contribution to the Critical Understanding of the Erasure of People from the Register of Permanent Residents of the Republic of Slovenia*. Ljubljana: Peace Institute.

Lacan, J. (1998 [1975]) *Encore: The Seminar of Jacques Lacan, Book XX, on Feminine Sexuality, The Limits of Love and Sexuality 1972–1973*. Ed. Miller, J.-A., trans Fink, B. New York: W.W. Norton.

Laclau, E. & Mouffe, C. (1985) *Hegemony and Socialist Strategy: Towards a Radical Democratic Politics*. London: Verso.

Lazić, M. (ed.) (1999) *Protest in Belgrade: Winter of Discontent*. Budapest: Central European University Press.

Lenin, V.I. (1968 [1917]) The State and Revolution. In *Selected Works*. Moscow: Progress Publishers.

Levi, P. (2007) *Disintegration in Frames: Aesthetics and Ideology in the Yugoslav and Post-Yugoslav Cinema*. Stanford, CA: Stanford University Press.

Magaš, B. (1989) The Spectre of Balkanization. *New Left Review* (I) 174. pp. 3–31.

Magaš, B. (1993) *The Destruction of Yugoslavia—Tracking the Break Up 1980–92*. London: Verso.

Močnik, R. (2006) On the Margins of Europe: An Interview. *Prelom* 8: 39–56.

Parker, I. (2004) *Slavoj Žižek: A Critical Introduction*. London: Pluto Press.

Pupovac, O. (2006) Springtime for Hegemony: Laclau and Mouffe with Janez Janša. *Prelom* 8: 115–135.

Williams, E.C. (2011) Review of *Lenin Reloaded: Towards a Politics of Truth*. *Historical Materialism: Research in Critical Marxist Theory* 19(3): 157–175.

Woodward, S.L. (1995) *The Balkan Tragedy: Chaos and Dissolution after the Cold War*. Washington, DC: Brookings Institution Press.

Wright, E.O. (2010) *Envisioning Real Utopias*. London: Verso.

Žižek, S. (1996a) Postscript. In Osborne, P. (ed.) *A Critical Sense: Interviews with Intellectuals*. London: Routledge.

Žižek, S. (1996b) Civil Society, Fanaticism, and Digital Reality: A Conversation with Slavoj Žižek. Interview with Lovink, G. www.ctheory.net/articles.aspx?id=79 (accessed 23 June 2010).

Žižek, S. (1999) Against the Double Blackmail. www.balkanwitness.glypx.com (accessed 19 July 2013).

Žižek, S. (2000) Repeating Lenin. www.lacan.com/replenin.htm (accessed 1 July 2010).

Žižek, S. (ed.) (2002) *Revolution at the Gates: Selected Writings of Lenin from 1917*. London: Verso.

Žižek, S. (2003) A Symptom—of What? *Critical Inquiry* 29 (Spring): 486–503.

Žižek, S. (2005) Some Politically Incorrect Reflections on Violence in France and Related Matters. www.lacan.com/zizfrance.htm (accessed 4 June 2010).

Žižek, S. (2006) *The Parallax View*. Cambridge, MA: MIT Press.

Žižek, S. (2007) Afterword: With Defenders Like These, Who Needs Attackers. In Bowman, P. & Stamp, R., *The Truth of Žižek*. London: Continuum.

Žižek, S. (2009a) *First as Tragedy, Then as Farce*. London: Verso.

Žižek, S. (2009b) *In Defense of Lost Causes*. London: Verso.

Žižek, S. (2010a) *Living in the End Times*. London: Verso.

Žižek, S. (2010b) Liberal Multiculturalism Masks an Old Barbarism with a Human Face. *The Guardian*. 3 October. www.guardian.co.uk (accessed 4 October 2010).

Žižek, S. (2010c) Some Concluding Notes on Violence, Ideology and Communist Culture. *Subjectivity* 3(1): 101–116.

Žižek, S. (2015a) The Non-Existence of Norway. *London Review of Books*, 9 September. www.lrb.co.uk/2015/09/09/slavoj-zizek/the-non-existence-of-norway (accessed 23 November 2015).

Žižek, S. (2015b) In the Wake of Paris Attacks the Left Must Embrace Its Radical Roots. *In These Times*, 16 November. http://inthesetimes.com/article/18605/breaking-the-taboos-in-the-wake-of-paris-attacks-the-left-must-embrace-its (accessed 23 November 2015).

Žižek, S. (2011) Message of Support. greekleftreview.wordpress.com/2011/02/18/no-human-is-illegal/ (accessed 10 April 2011).

Žižek, S. & Salecl, R. (1996) Lacan in Slovenia: Slavoj Žižek and Renata Salecl. Interview with Dews, P. & Osborne, P. In Osborne, P. (ed.) *A Critical Sense: Interviews with Intellectuals*. London: Routledge.

Zorn, J. (2009) Slovenia: Ethnic Exclusion in a Model Accession State. In Rechel, B. (ed.) *Minority Rights in Central and Eastern Europe*. London: Routledge.

Zorn, J. & Čebron, U.L. (2008) *Once Upon an Erasure: From Citizens to Illegal Residents in the Republic of Slovenia*. Ljubljana: Peace Institute.

PART II
Radicalizing Žižek

INTRODUCTION
Thinking through Žižek and beyond

Žižek has responded in print to some of the criticisms I make in the first part of this book and I want to pick up on one remark here:

> To put it with some irony, I do not even agree with Homer where Homer agrees with me: he refers approvingly to my endorsement of Alain Badiou's motto, "Those who are here are from here," which seems to me now problematic, at least in its abstract form—as I was reminded during a visit to the West Bank, every Jewish settler would have whole-heartedly supported this motto.
> *(Žižek 2013, p. 771, note 1)*

How is one to respond to this response? Badiou's slogan, as I understand it, was developed to address the issue of immigration and the discrimination against migrants in Europe and elsewhere. I fail to see how it applies to an occupying force. If Jewish settlers occupying Palestinian territory on the West Bank were to adopt this slogan, then once again I would agree with Žižek. Although I am sure he would find further grounds to disagree with me. However, this is not what the slogan refers to. It has no meaning in this context. Politically I cannot see how we can "get serious" and rebuild the left in the region if we just throw around a few slogans that appeal to us and drop them a year or two later. The left needs, as Badiou would put it, an affirmative project that outlines an alternative to the current conjuncture of neo-liberal austerity. Žižek's work can often provide us with an incisive critique of the socio-ideological fantasy that sustains this conjuncture but not a way out of it. In this sense Žižek's ongoing dialogue with Alain Badiou is instructive.

Today, argues Žižek, one must "think through Lacan, go further than he did, but the only way beyond Lacan is through Lacan" (Žižek 2012a, p. 18). Any radical emancipatory project he concludes must remain faithful to this fundamental insight of Badiou's and pass through Lacan. In Part II of this book I suggest that any assessment of Žižek's own radical project must think through his engagement with Badiou and go beyond Žižek. Every major work that Žižek has published since *The Ticklish Subject* (1999) has contained an extended presentation and critique of Badiou. Indeed, Badiou's current stature in the Anglophone academy is in no small part thanks to Žižek's explication of his ideas in a series of works in the late 1990s (Žižek 1998, 1999), and Žižek's Pauline turn in the early 2000s (Žižek 2000, 2003) drew freely on Badiou's *Saint Paul: The Foundation of Universalism*. Žižek's endorsement of revolutionary terror (Žižek 2009b, pp. 157–210) was extensively informed by Badiou's work and his notion of an authentic political act has been subtly transformed under the influence of Badiou. As with his other major interlocutors, Ernesto Laclau and Judith Butler, Žižek has consistently sought to present his own position as a radicalization of Badiou's work.

Chapter 4 thus traces the trajectory of Žižek's critique of Badiou and, more specifically, his rhetorical strategy of reformulating Badiou's theoretical positions in order to undercut them with his own Lacanian critique. Furthermore, thinking through Badiou, and what is often referred to as his affirmationism, we can identify the theoretical basis for a consistent emancipatory politics that is lacking in Žižek's negative gesture of "wiping the slate clean."

In Chapter 5 I explore how Badiou's politics and his more measured assessment of the necessity of violence offers an antidote to some of Žižek's more reckless statements on the issue. Considering Žižek's statements on political violence in the context of the anti-austerity riots in Greece, the rise of urban guerrilla groups and, finally, the increase in fascist violence from Golden Dawn, I argue that such "negative gestures" are counter-productive and result in lasting political damage to the left. First, I will explore a slightly different aspect of Žižek's politics of negation, again through the Greek crisis—that is to say, his notion of the "radical refusal" or Bartleby politics.

Bartleby politics and the Greek crisis

What is radical about Bartleby's "I would prefer not to," argues Žižek, is precisely that "it is a signifier-turned object, a signifier reduced to an inert stain that stands for the collapse of the symbolic order" (Žižek 2006, p. 385). So, doing nothing does *not* mean simply doing nothing, but doing nothing in order to bring capitalism to its knees! For Žižek, Bartleby is exemplary of the radical refusal:

> In his refusal of the Master's order, Bartleby does not negate the predicate; rather, he affirms a non-predicate: he does not say that he *doesn't want to do it*; he says that *he prefers (wants) not to do it*. This is how we pass from the politics of "resistance" or "protestation," which parasitizes upon what it negates, to a politics which opens up a new space outside the hegemonic position *and* its negation.
>
> *(Žižek 2006, pp. 381–82, emphasis in the original)*

This is the gesture of *subtraction* at its purest in the sense that it is not just a negation but a "negation of the negation," and therefore offers the possibility of a new opening. However, in what sense can we say that Bartleby's refusal is an opening to something new?

Fabio Vighi and Heiko Feldner (2010) elucidate the implications of Bartleby politics in relation to the ongoing global financial crisis, and their presentation is particularly useful insofar as Žižek has endorsed it as exemplary of what he means by Bartleby politics (Žižek 2010b, p. 101). For Vighi and Feldner, Bartleby politics involves not simply doing nothing but a strategic withdrawal "to exert pressure on the points of suture in order to undermine the libidinal economy of the very system from which it withdraws" (Vighi & Feldner 2010, p. 44). If we look at the responses to the bailout packages that were immediately put in place when the financial meltdown engulfed the banks in 2008 we can see they fall into two main groups. On the one hand, we have a range of responses from outright rejection ("road to socialism") to cynicism ("the worse the better"), exemplified through the writings of Naomi Klein, and on the other, there is an unconditional embrace ("state intervention at all cost") characterized by Vighi and Feldner as "*neoliberal Keynesianism*" (ibid., p. 48, emphasis in the original).

Drawing on Žižek's own analysis of the financial crisis, Vighi and Feldner argue that what Klein's position of outright rejection fails to address is the fact that the effect of the "rescue packages" is real and effective and the alternative would be much worse (Vighi & Feldner 2010, p. 45). Furthermore, again taking their cue from Žižek, they argue that as long as we are stuck with capitalism then the trickle-down argument contains a grain of truth: "the collapse of Wall Street really will hit ordinary workers."

This brings Vighi and Feldner to their second argument, that to blame the bankers and financial speculators as the central causal agents of the current dilemma, while understandable, "is politically misleading and factually wrong" (Vighi & Feldner 2010, p. 46). The bankers and financial speculators were simply doing what they do, behaving like good capitalists and making profit. How does Bartleby politics help us negotiate this dilemma?

> Bartleby's politics of subtraction … does not mean to abstain from direct engagement in the system but *to resist the urge to merely resist* (performing a blocking action). It means to refrain from forms of participation in the hegemonic practices and rituals that function as their inherent supplement and are expected of leftist resistance.
>
> *(Vighi & Feldner 2010, p. 48, emphasis in the original)*

In short, we must resist facile calls to reject the bailouts and return to state intervention through nationalization of the banks and the regulation of financial markets as these measures will only serve to shore up a system in crisis. We should rather support realistic "sustainable solutions [that] take into account the deep systemic roots of the unfolding ecological catastrophe" which are concealed by the rampant economic crisis (Vighi & Feldner 2010, p. 49).

I do not entirely disagree, but this is not exactly a radical agenda. I also wonder how a Bartleby approach helps us here, rather than Badiou's proposal that we should not only reject the false choice offered to us but also *affirm* an alternative (Badiou & Žižek 2009, p. 89). Following Žižek, Vighi and Feldner present us with two alternatives from cynicism on the one hand to neo-liberal Keynesianism on the other, and suggest that we refuse both alternatives in favor of more realistic and sustainable solutions. However, this is a false choice. There always was and remains a radical left response to the financial crisis that rejects both of the above positions and fully understands the consequences of a sovereign default, but still affirms that position.[1]

Indeed, if Greece had unilaterally defaulted in 2010 the major French and German banks would have been severely hit, as would the Greek banks that held the majority of the debt. The purpose of the eurozone bailouts was to transfer this debt from the private banks to the Greek state, which it successfully did over the following two years. At the time the left of SYRIZA (the Coalition of the Radical Left and Movements) was under no illusions that to default on the debt was to default on its own banks and pension funds, but at least this would give the country a chance to recover economically in five to ten years rather than the perpetual low growth and restricted spending to which the country is now resigned. The radical left affirmed such a position precisely so that Greeks could take back control of their own state, their own economy and their own lives, but it was under no illusions that this would be easy or solve all of the country's problems. This was also a position that many on the left assumed, at least until the European elections of 2012, that SYRIZA maintained.

Seize the moment; well, maybe not!

Žižek has been a prominent supporter of SYRIZA since the beginning of the eurozone crisis in the autumn of 2009, regularly sharing a platform with Alexis Tsipras and Yannis Varoufakis and giving talks in Athens. Despite SYRIZA's populism, which increased markedly after the party's success in the 2012 European elections, and the corresponding dilution of their more radical proposals, Žižek has remained consistent in his view that the Greek left offered the last best hope for a European emancipatory project. As Žižek writes in *The Year of Dreaming Dangerously* (2012b), SYRIZA represented a real alternative to the European establishment; it represented all that was worth saving in Europe— democracy, trust in the people and egalitarian solidarity. In short, "Greece is … Europe's singular universality: the nodal point at which the historical tendency that shapes its present appears at its purest" (Žižek 2012b, p. 15). Žižek concludes his reflections on the dangerous dreams of emancipation with his now familiar exhortations to reject the future as catastrophe and embrace the future as possibility and openness to the new. One might expect, therefore, that SYRIZA's dramatic U-turn after the referendum of 5 July 2015 and subsequent capitulation to the Troika (the Eurozone Group, the European Central Bank and the International Monetary Fund) would result in something of a crisis of faith for Žižek but this has not been the case.

In an article entitled "The Courage of Hopelessness" (2015a),[2] Žižek argued in support of SYRIZA:

> The true courage is not to imagine an alternative, but to accept the consequences of the fact that there is no clearly discernible alternative: the dream of an alternative is a sign of theoretical cowardice; it functions as a fetish that prevents us thinking through to the end of the deadlock of our predicament.
>
> *(Žižek 2015a, n.p.)*

While the "no" in the referendum was a great "ethico-political act," an "authentic gesture of freedom and autonomy," the startling U-turn by SYRIZA is not to be understood as a failure, a betrayal of its left ideals but rather a failure of Europe itself, "of the emancipatory core of the European Legacy." Indeed, the "no" of the referendum could survive if SYRIZA leads a patient guerrilla war against European financial occupation. For Žižek the battle was already lost when the problem was posed as a choice between a "Grexit" and capitulation to Brussels as this false choice remains within the predominant Eurocentric horizon. SYRIZA had no choice, we are told; there is no outside of the eurozone for a small country like Greece and therefore SYRIZA made the only decision it could: to accept the dictates of Brussels. The only thing left is for SYRIZA to act with "ruthless pragmatism and cold calculation, it should exploit the tiniest cracks in the opponent's armour" (Žižek 2015a, n.p.). What of the left of SYRIZA, those members of parliament who refused to accept the third bailout? For Žižek they have been relegated to the "so-called 'left'" who are accused of "empty posturing" because they refuse to accept the responsibility of governing and taking over state power.

In a follow-up article addressing his critics, "The Greek Apocalypse: Versailles or Brest-Litovsk?" (Žižek 2015b), Žižek elaborated on the issue of controlling state power further:

> We are not at the end. The Greek retreat is not the last word for the simple reason that the crisis will hit again, in a couple of years if not sooner, and not only in Greece. The task of the Syriza government is to get ready for that moment, to patiently occupy positions and plan options. Holding onto political power in these impossible conditions nonetheless provides a minimal space to prepare the ground for future action and for political education.
>
> *(Žižek 2015b, n.p.)*

Controlling the state apparatus, along with its 2 million employees,[3] argues Žižek, will allow SYRIZA to prepare for the next, inevitable, eruption of the crisis. Critics such as Stathis Gourgouris and Tariq Ali, who accuse SYRIZA of a "betrayal," are once again summarily dismissed for taking the easy option and refusing to confront the truly big questions: How does one confront capital? How does one govern and run the state today? SYRIZA refused the false choice between a true heroic act and a betrayal and made "an actual difficult choice" that must now be enacted with "brutal pragmatic terms" (Žižek 2015b, n.p.).

The problem for many of us as we watch SYRIZA take control of the state apparatus and implement some of the harshest austerity measures the country has yet seen is that it is hard to distinguish what they are doing from the usual business of clientelism in Greece. It is also very difficult to reconcile the policies the SYRIZA government are implementing with any notion of a patient guerrilla war against financial occupation. SYRIZA promised the Greek electorate a fairer and more socially just distribution of austerity measures, but to date their alternative measures and parallel program have failed to materialize and their current policies of cutting public spending, reducing pensions and increasing taxes on salaried workers is very much in line with the two previous governments. Indeed, the situation is more than a little absurd when the government calls for consensus amongst the established political parties and, at the same time, calls its own supporters out on strike against the very measures that it is passing through parliament.[4]

So, is Žižek right? Must we accept that there was no other choice but to be brutally pragmatic and now hold on to state power at all costs? In the spring of 2015 Costas Lapavitsas and Heiner Flassbeck drafted the "Program of Social and National Rescue for Greece":

> The program thus put forth an integrated set of measures that constituted an alternative policy: writing off debt, rejecting balanced budgets, nationalizing banks, redistributing income and wealth through tax reform, raising the minimum wage, restoring labor regulation, boosting public investment, and redesigning the relationship between the private and the public sector.
>
> *(Lapavitsas 2015, n.p.)*

Although the program was not published until after the September 2015 election, it gives the lie to Tsipras's argument that there was no alternative. Žižek is fully aware of this alternative but dismisses it as the "usual set of state-interventionist measures" (Žižek 2015b) that could possibly work but is unlikely to do so, given that Greece is now fully integrated into, and dependent upon, Western European markets. There is no "outside" of Europe for Greece to turn to; if Greece defaults it will be socially and economically isolated. These are the questions, observes Žižek, that the members of SYRIZA who went on to found Popular Unity "have yet to address." It is certainly possible that state intervention will not work in Greece, but whatever happened to Žižek's radical rhetoric of "we are the ones we have been waiting for" (Žižek 2009a, p. 148), and "trust in the people" (Žižek 2009b, p. 461)?

The alternative offered by the left in Greece is once again to reject the false choice offered by the eurozone and the Greek establishment, of which SYRIZA is now a part, and for Greeks to take back control of their own lives and economy. Once again Žižek has taken sides with those in power and in control of the state, dismissing those who want to retain a principled opposition and resistance to eurozone austerity measures as naive and misguided idealists who do not want to get their hands dirty with the practical business of running a country.

Notes

1 Costas Lapavitsas, the most prominent Marxist economist from SYRIZA's Left Platform, now the Popular Unity Party, has advocated unilateral default and return to a national currency since the onset of the crisis. See his co-authored reports for the Research on Money and Finance Group (Lapavitsas et al. 2010a; 2010b).

2 The article was first published in the *New Statesman* (20 July 2015) and was reprinted in *In These Times* on 23 July 2015 with the title "How Alexis Tsipras and Syriza Outmanoeuvred Angela Merkel and the Eurocrats." Žižek did not consent to the change of title which gave the piece a much more optimistic tone.

3 I am not sure where Žižek gets the figure of 2 million state employees from, the Greek government admits that it does not know exactly how many employees there are in the public sector but usually sets the figure below 1 million.

4 This was the case with the first general strike called against SYRIZA on 12 November 2015.

References

Badiou, A. & Žižek, S. (2009) *Philosophy in the Present*. Ed. Engelmann, P., trans. Thomas, P. & Toscano, A. Cambridge: Polity Press.

Lapavitsas, C. (2015) The Path Not Taken. *Jacobin*. 10 September. www.jacobinmag.com/2015/10/greece-debt-tsipras-eurozone-syriza-draghi/ (accessed 30 November 2015).

Lapavitsas, C., Kaltenbrunner, A., Lindo, D., Michell, J., Painceira, J.P., Pires, E., Powell, J., Stenfors, A. & Teles, N. (2010a) Eurozone Crisis: Beggar Thyself and Thy Neighbor. *Journal of Balkan and Near Eastern Studies* 12(4): 321–372.

Lapavitsas, C., Kaltenbrunner, A., Lindo, D., Michell, J., Painceira, J.P., Pires, E., Powell, J., Stenfors, A. & Teles, N. (2010b) *The Eurozone Between Austerity and Default*. www.researchonmoneyandfinance.org/images/other_papers/RMF-Eurozone-Austerity-and-Default.pdf (accessed 16 March 2016).

Vighi, F. & Feldner, H. (2010) From Subject to Politics: The Žižekian Field Today. *Subjectivity* 3(1): 31–52.

Žižek, S. (1998) Psychoanalysis in Post-Marxism: The Case of Alain Badiou. Psycho-Marxism: Marxism and Psychoanalysis Late in the Twentieth Century. *The South Atlantic Quarterly* 97(2): 235–261.

Žižek, S. (1999) *The Ticklish Subject: The Absent Centre of Political Ontology*. London: Verso.

Žižek, S. (2000) *The Fragile Absolute—or, Why is the Christian Legacy Worth Fighting For?* London: Verso.

Žižek, S. (2003) *The Puppet and the Dwarf: The Perverse Core of Christianity*. Cambridge, MA: MIT Press.

Žižek, S. (2006) *The Parallax View*. Cambridge, MA: MIT Press.

Žižek, S. (2009a) *First as Tragedy, Then as Farce*. London: Verso.

Žižek, S. (2009b) *In Defense of Lost Causes*. London: Verso.

Žižek, S. (2010a) *Living in the End Times*. London: Verso.

Žižek, S. (2010b) Some Concluding Notes on Violence, Ideology and Communist Culture. *Subjectivity* 3(1): 101–116.

Žižek, S. (2012a) *Less Than Nothing: Hegel and the Shadow of Dialectical Materialism*. London: Verso.

Žižek, S. (2012b) *The Year of Dreaming Dangerously*. London: Verso.

Žižek, S. (2013) Reply. *Slavic Review: Interdisciplinary Quarterly of Russian, Eurasian, and East European Studies* 72(4): 771–777.

Žižek, S. (2015a) The Courage of Hopelessness. *The New Statesman*. 20 July. www.newstatesman.com/world-affairs/2015/07/slavoj-i-ek-greece-course-hopelessness (accessed 26 July 2015).

Žižek, S. (2015b) The Greek Apocalypse: Versailles or Brest-Litovsk? *In These Times*. 24 August. inthesetimes.com/article/18339/the-greek-apocalypse-versailles-or-brest-litovsk (accessed 30 November 2015).

4

THE POLITICS OF COMRADESHIP

Philosophical commitment and construction in Alain Badiou and Slavoj Žižek

Alain Badiou and Slavoj Žižek concluded a 2009 philosophical dialogue with a declaration of their solidarity and "comradeship" (Badiou & Žižek 2009, p. 104). Badiou, however, introduces a qualification: their dialogue centers on forms of philosophical commitment and their mutual agreement is all the greater for it, but if they were to broach the question of philosophical construction, then differences would certainly open up between them. Badiou highlights their respective notions of the event, the real, the function of the imaginary and, finally, politics as a decision or process (ibid., p. 101). Contrary to the tenor of our age, Badiou is a systematic thinker; philosophy, he argues, involves the organization, the configuration, of concepts around the category of Truth. A Truth (with a capital T) "is by itself *void*," it "operates but presents nothing" (Badiou 1999, p. 124, emphasis in the original), and as such, as an operational void, it facilitates the gathering together, or compossibility, of local truths. Philosophy, therefore, does not produce truth but constructs procedures to "seize truths" (ibid., p. 127). Philosophy in this sense is not the interpretation of experience, but the act of constructing truth or generic procedures that stand out from the cumulative fields of knowledge by their novelty, their eventful origin (ibid., p. 36).

Žižek, by contrast, is known for his digressive, unsystematic and omnivorous style. If Badiou is precise in his definition of concepts and his construction of philosophy's four generic procedures—i.e. art, love, politics and science—then Žižek is often frustratingly loose in his deployment of concepts. He does, however, repeatedly return to the same philosophical and political debates with key interlocutors. In this chapter I will draw out the main threads of Žižek's critique of his longstanding friend and comrade Alain Badiou.

The dialogue between Žižek and Badiou has been rather one-sided as far as the published texts go. Since *The Ticklish Subject* (1999), each of Žižek's major publications has engaged with Badiou's work. In *The Ticklish Subject* Žižek argued that his primary difference with Badiou centered on their divergent understandings of the Lacanian real and the drive. For Žižek, every authentic political act is grounded upon an initial negative gesture, insofar as the act is a repetition of the subject's "forced" entry into the symbolic order, and he contrasts this with Badiou's politics of affirmation and the "pure event." *The Parallax View* (2006) restates this critique, arguing that the death drive is the materialist support for Badiou's "positive infinity." *The Parallax View* also shifts the focus of Žižek's critique to political economy, arguing that this is the major weakness of Badiou's system and politics. *In Defense of Lost Causes* (2009b) provides Žižek's first sustained reading of Badiou's *Logics of Worlds: Being and Event II* (2009a), and once more he focuses on the function of the death drive and Badiou's concept of "subtraction." From Žižek's perspective the problem with the politics of subtraction—taking a distance from the state but not destroying it—is that it represents a negative gesture but not a "determinate negation." In his *magnum opus*, *Less Than Nothing* (2012), Žižek further develops his critique of *Logics of Worlds*, arguing in a threefold critique that Badiou lacks "an ontology of the Event" (Žižek 2012, p. 805). *Less Than Nothing* also presents Žižek's first sustained engagement with Badiou's Lacanian-inflected *Theory of the Subject* (2009b). Underlying all of these exchanges are Badiou and Žižek's respective understandings of the void, or gap, and its relation to the subject. Badiou argues that the subject is extremely rare, emerging only through a fidelity to the event, while for Žižek the subject is the void or gap, "a Nothingness counted as Something" (Žižek 1998, p. 256). In short, argues Žižek, are we to understand the relationship between void and subject in a properly dialectical, Hegelian manner or from a neo-Kantian perspective?

Badiou has hardly responded to Žižek's criticisms in print. In a rare comment on their relationship he describes it as "a politburo of the two," the only question being who will shoot whom first, "after having wrung from him a deeply felt self-criticism" (Badiou 2009a, p. 563). Bruno Bosteels has suggested that Badiou's silence in this respect may be a consequence of the blurring of exegesis and critique in Žižek's work. In his view, "what presents itself as a straight forward summary of Badiou's philosophy is already heavily influenced and refracted by Žižek's own thought," while his counter-arguments are often faithful paraphrases of Badiou's ideas rewritten in Lacanese (Bosteels 2005, p. 225). This often makes it difficult to disentangle Žižek's critique, as his solutions to the aporias of Badiou's crypto-Kantianism frequently appear to be remarkably similar to Badiou's own position. Bosteels notes that Žižek's criticisms fall into three categories: psychoanalytic, philosophical and political. While it is impossible to separate these three areas of criticism, as each directly implicates the others, I will broadly follow these distinctions below.

Circumventing psychoanalysis: Between two deaths

Žižek's first explication of Badiou's work appeared in *The South Atlantic Quarterly* (1998) as "Psychoanalysis in Post-Marxism: The Case of Alain Badiou."[1] Žižek elaborates a Lacanian critique of Badiou in relation to the real, the death drive and the subject which has remained constant. Badiou's circumvention of psychoanalysis, argues Žižek, derives from his homology between Christianity and Marxism and specifically his Pauline turn. Badiou inverts the usual opposition between the law and grace, whereby we are all subject to divine law and the elect are touched by grace. Furthermore, the law is particular and grace universal. Corresponding to the two lives (the finite biological life and the eternal life promised through grace) are two deaths (biological death and the death through sin):

> The direct result of the intervention of the Law is thus to *divide* the subject, introducing a morbid confusion between life and death, between the (conscious) obedience of the law and the (unconscious) desire for its transgression that is *generated by the legal prohibition*.
>
> (*Žižek 1998, p. 249, emphasis in the original*)

The problem is how to break out of this vicious cycle of law and transgression, how to think transformation, and here Badiou introduces the cut of the event, the novelty of the resurrection as an "absolute disjunction."

There is, however, an alternative to this separation of death and resurrection, Lacan's insight into the domain "between two deaths," the domain of lamella.[2] In order to open oneself up to the true life of eternity, writes Žižek, "one's attachment to 'this' life must be suspended for entry into the domain ... between the two deaths, the domain of the 'undead'" (Žižek 1998, p. 247). The domain between the two deaths crystallizes, argues Žižek, the gap that separates Badiou from Lacan and psychoanalysis in general.[3] The only kind of fidelity one has from a Lacanian point of view is not to compromise on one's desire. There is no resolution or harmony to achieve but what Žižek calls "wiping the slate clean" (ibid., p. 252). It is this negative gesture of wiping the slate clean that creates the space for the arrival of the new and precedes any positive gesture of identification with a cause. In this sense, argues Žižek, Lacan implicitly shifts the balance between death and resurrection towards death. Death stands for:

> [T]he "night of the world," the self-withdrawal, the absolute contraction of subjectivity in which its very links with "reality" are severed—*this* is "wiping the slate clean," which opens up the domain of the symbolic New Beginning and enables the emergence of the "New Harmony" sustained by a newly emerged Master-Signifier.
>
> (*Žižek 1998, p. 253, emphasis in the original*)

In Lacanese every event remains a mere semblance, masking the prior void of the death drive. A "Truth-Event," argues Žižek, operates against this background of a traumatic encounter with the domain of the undead, with the real. The conflation and capitalization of truth and event by Žižek is precisely the blurring of exegesis and critique mentioned above. After presenting Badiou's theory in his own terms, Žižek then proceeds to critique a construct (the truth event) that is not in the original. Truth and event, for Badiou, remain distinct but related concepts; an event is a moment of opening through which the new can emerge, while truth is a generic procedure which retrospectively nominates an event. Through thinking the nature of their relation Badiou renders the domain of truth. I will come back to this below; first, however, I will address the issue of the death drive.

The death drive: Repetition or rupture

The principal difference between Žižek and Badiou regarding an authentic event turns on the death drive, or the primacy of negation for Žižek versus affirmation in Badiou. An event for Badiou emerges from a rupture in the order of being; it is an opening between one closure and another. Through a subject's fidelity to the truth of that moment of opening the event is retrospectively constituted. The French Revolution constitutes such an event: on the one hand, it was merely the sequence of traces or facts that took place between 1789 and 1794; on the other, it retrospectively became the *central term of the Revolution itself* (Badiou 2005a, p. 180). From Žižek's perspective, *the new can only emerge through repetition* (Žižek 2009a, p. 140). A revolution is exemplary of such a process, insofar as "the October Revolution repeated the French Revolution, redeeming its failure, unearthing and repeating the same impulse" (ibid., p. 139). Badiou's rejection of repetition derives from a critique of Lacan's structural dialectic. Lacan did not push his insight into the real far enough and consider that which exceeds the repetition compulsion of the signifying chain. Everything that repeats, writes Badiou, is invariably unjust and inexact, whereas justice and rightness are novelties (Badiou 2009b, p. 39). Žižek's failure to engage directly with Badiou's critique of Lacan until *Less Than Nothing* (2012) is telling, as this critique of psychoanalysis underpins his later work.

For Žižek, it is the repetition of the death drive that accounts for the emergence of novelty. He rejects, however, the traditional reading of the Freudian drive that links it to human biology and an organism's tendency to return to an inorganic state:

> The paradox of the Freudian "death drive" is therefore that it is Freud's name for its very opposite, for the way immortality appears within psychoanalysis, for an uncanny *excess* of life, for an "undead" urge which persists beyond the (biological) cycle of life and death, of generation and corruption. The ultimate lesson of psychoanalysis is that human life is never "just life": humans are not simply alive, they are possessed by the strange drive to enjoy

life in excess, passionately attached to a surplus which sticks out and derails the ordinary run of things.

(Žižek 2006, p. 62)

The death drive has nothing to do with a will to self-annihilation, but is the reason that this will is never realized and the subject gets "stuck" on partial objects. If the metonymy of desire is the infinite pursuit of a lost object, then the drive designates how desire becomes "fixated" or "stuck" on a specific object, "condemned to circulate around it forever" (Žižek 2006, p. 62).

It is the mute, repetitive, rotary motion of the drive, contends Žižek, which is primary and ultimately the *groundless* ground of human freedom (Žižek 1996, pp. 32–35). The death drive is beyond human mortality; it is a "vanishing mediator" between being and event, or the mortality of the individual and the immortality of the subject. As Adrian Johnston (2009) puts it, the death drive "is a name for subjectivity qua the void of a radical negativity irreducible to any and every form of positive inscription or representation" (ibid., p. 157). The death drive facilitates Žižek's distinction between the subject as void, as pure negativity, as nothing, and what he calls *subjectification*—in Badiou's sense of a subject-of-the-event—as secondary to this moment of pure negativity. The elementary act of freedom, then, is negation. It is saying "no" to the big Other; it is breaking out of the closed repetitive circuit of the death drive and asserting a minimal distance, a parallax gap, between the real and the symbolic. The radicalism of the Freudian drive lies in this negativity behind all affirmation. The death drive is a self-sabotaging structure and the minimum prerequisite for subjective freedom. In this sense the death drive decenters the subject and opens up the minimal space for a subject to act.

Bruno Bosteels (2011) has convincingly argued that in order to understand Badiou's affirmationism adequately we must situate it in relation to his formulation of destruction in *Theory of the Subject* (2009b). Lacan, famously, was unable to comprehend the revolutionary upheavals of May 1968 and to see anything positive in the movement beyond the hysterical demand for a new master (Lacan 1990, p. 126). For Badiou, the fundamental impasse of Lacanian psychoanalysis and its weakness in thinking political transformation lies with its conception of lack and the real. In order to move beyond the impasse of the lacking subject and confer a degree of consistency upon it that would allow us to think radical change as well as the emergence of novelty beyond the repetition of the past, we must think lack with destruction. Every subject, writes Badiou, "stands at a crossing between a lack of being and a destruction, a repetition and an interruption, a placement and an excess" (Badiou 2009b, p. 139). It is at this intersection of lack and destruction that something emerges, "an other of the Other, from which it follows that what functioned as the first Other now appears as nothing more than an unenlightened mode of the Same" (ibid., p. 156). Badiou's notion of destruction beyond the law of lack "consists precisely in the capacity to bring into being the nonrepeatable within repetition," to bring about the new (Bosteels 2011, p. 101). In a self-critique of his "misguided" use of the theme of destruction Badiou later restricts the concept to "a supplementation by a truth," destruction is of the order of knowledge but is not true (Badiou 2005a, pp. 407–8). Badiou clarifies this in his discussion of the Paris Commune. The commune event did not set out merely to destroy the political elite—to wipe the slate clean in Žižek's terms—but to do something more radical: it sought the destruction of "the political subordination of the workers and the people" (Badiou 2009a, p. 379). The commune destroyed "the order of subjective incapacity," as the inexistence of the proletariat came into existence. Badiou's more measured appreciation of negation and destruction, I believe, provides a useful antidote to the valorization of negation and violence in Žižek. As the drive in Lacan is inextricably tied to the real, the debate between Žižek and Badiou essentially turns on their respective understanding and deployment of this concept.

Splitting the real

Žižek has undoubtedly done more than any other contemporary theorist to reorient our understanding of Lacan around the concept of the real. In his early work he stressed the impossibility of the real, the real as an impenetrable kernel resisting symbolization, and insisted on the necessity of maintaining the gap separating the real and the symbolic (Žižek 1989, p. 3). From this perspective, "*the only point at which we approach this hard kernel of the Real is indeed the dream*" or symptom (ibid., p. 47, emphasis in the original). Over the years Žižek's deployment of the real has changed but, as with Lacan, he never completely abandons his prior formulations.

In his debate with Judith Butler and Ernesto Laclau, Žižek identified the real with capital, insofar as the real marks the absolute limit to resignification. Moreover, he began suggesting the possibility of "touching" the real, when the symbolic markers that distance us from it are suspended (Butler et al. 2000, p. 223). In *The Parallax View* Žižek distinguishes between the Lacanian real and the "parallax real," as "the disavowed X on account of which our vision of reality is anamorphically distorted; it is simultaneously the Thing to which direct access is not possible and the obstacle which prevents this direct access, the Thing which eludes our grasp and the distorting screen which makes us miss the Thing" (Žižek 2006, p. 26). The parallax real is not the Lacanian real that "always remains in its place," and neither is it the hard impenetrable kernel beyond the symbolic. The parallax real is the gap itself, the gap that renders two perspectives radically *incommensurable* (ibid., p. 281). The impossibility of the real is now conceptualized as "the cause of the impossibility of ever attaining the 'neutral' non perspectival view of the object." In other words, the Lacanian real is not only the distorted object but the principle of distortion itself, and in this sense the real is *within* the symbolic (Žižek 2009b, p. 319). Today, Žižek argues that the real is not an abyss that forever eludes our grasp or an inaccessible Thing, but "the *gap* which presents our access to it" (Žižek 2004, p. 168), and it is this real, he contends, that Badiou fails to grasp in his opposition of being and event:

> The ultimate difference between Badiou and Lacan thus concerns the relationship between the shattering encounter with the Real and the ensuing arduous work of transforming this explosion of negativity into a new order. For Badiou, this new order "sublates" the exploding negativity into a new consistent truth, while for Lacan every Truth displays the structure of a (symbolic) fiction, i.e. no Truth is able to touch the Real.
>
> *(Žižek 2004, p. 177)*

In order to forestall the charge of postmodern relativism Žižek invokes the notion of the real in all three of Lacan's orders—the imaginary, the symbolic, the real—and in a strictly homologous way he invokes three modalities of the real within the symbolic. "Far from being reduced to the traumatic void of the Thing which resists symbolisation," writes Žižek, "the Lacanian Real thus designates also the senseless symbolic consistency (of the 'matheme'), as well as the pure appearance irreducible to its causes ('the real of an illusion')" (Žižek 2004, p. 177). The real appears to have become an infinitely malleable concept.

In a brief footnote to *Logics of Worlds* (2009a) Badiou argues that Žižek's conception of the real is "so ephemeral, so brutally punctual, that it is impossible to uphold its consequences." He continues: "The effects of this kind of frenzied upsurge, in which the real rules over the comedy of our symptoms, are ultimately indiscernible from skepticism" (Badiou 2009a, p. 563). There are two notions of the real in Lacan, according to Badiou: first, the structural understanding of the real as a vanishing cause or the lack of being, and second, the late topological Lacan that gives a minimum of consistency to the real, as the being of lack (Badiou 2009b, pp. 132–9). Lacan's insight was the role of the real as antagonism, as that which always already fissures the social and means that it can never be rendered whole or complete. However, if we think the real only in this way, then we remain caught within the totality of the structure itself and cannot think its potential transformation. Lacan's "materialist" dialectic is only half the picture; we must not only think the real as impossible, unbearable trauma but also as something that, on rare occasions, becomes the site for a newly consistent truth—that is to say, the real as novelty:

> The line of demarcation between idealism and materialism in Lacan's thought must therefore be drawn through the very concept of the real, splitting its core in order to mark off those aspects that remain tied to a structural lack and those that point at a torsion, or destruction, of the structure itself.
>
> *(Bosteels 2011, p. 87)*

In *Theory of the Subject*, Badiou develops this idea through the concept of forcing: it is not enough merely to expose the lack, the absent cause; we must also force or distort the real in order "to give consistency to the real as a new generic truth" (Bosteels 2011, p. 88). In other words, it is not enough merely to think the subject as lack, we must also think it as excess. The theory of the subject is complete only when "it manages to think the structural law of the empty place as the punctual anchoring of the excess over the place" (Badiou 2009b, p. 261). In short, we have two opposing views of the subject, the subject as consistent repetition, in which the real ex-sists (Lacan), and the subject as destructive consistency, in which the real ex-ceeds (Badiou 2009b, p. 239). Whilst this might not be strictly Lacanian, it does have the advantage of allowing us to think radical structural change in ways foreclosed by Lacan himself.

Philosophy: Mind the gap

For Žižek, the central axis of Badiou's theoretical edifice is the *gap* between being and event, and it is this gap that he will repeatedly pry apart in his critique of Badiou's non-dialectical separation of being and event, subject and subjectivization, truth and knowledge, representation and presentation, facilitating his final charge of Kantian formalism. From his initial explication of Badiou, Žižek has consistently presented an event as external, beyond, or in opposition to the order of being. In the proto-Kantian opposition between the positive order of being and the radical unconditional demand for a "Truth-Event" lies Badiou's fatal weakness (Žižek 1998, p. 259). An authentic event, insists Žižek, is something that emerges *ex nihilo* and is the truth of a situation that makes visible what the official discourse has had to repress. Furthermore, it "does not entail any ontological guarantee" but a *decision* of a committed, engaged subject (ibid., p. 240). In Lacanese, "Event is *objet a*, while denomination is the new signifier that establishes ... the new readability of the situation on the basis of Decision" (ibid., p. 242). Whilst the presentation of the event as "creation *ex nihilo*" is crucial for Žižek's identification of an event with Lacan's act, it is not strictly speaking Badiou's formulation:

> [A]s far as its material is concerned, the event is not a miracle. What I mean is that what composes an event is always extracted from a situation, always related back to a singular multiplicity, to its state, to the language that is connected to it, etc. In fact, if we want to avoid lapsing into an obscurantist theory of creation *ex-nihilo*, we must accept that an event is nothing but a part of a given situation, nothing but a *fragment of being*.
> *(Badiou 2004, p. 98)*

Commenting on this passage, Žižek reiterates that there is a fundamental ambiguity within Badiou's ontology—that is, "how do Event and Being relate ontologically" (Žižek 2009c, p. 212). Žižek restates this Kantian reading of Badiou in *Less Than Nothing*, where he insists that Badiou's Event is "break in the order of being (transcendentally constituted phenomenal reality), the intrusion of a radically heterogeneous ('noumenal') order" (Žižek 2012, p. 185). In short, Badiou's systematic philosophy, as it is expounded in *Logics of Worlds*, is nothing less than "Kantianism reinvented for the epoch of radical contingency" (ibid., p. 185). For Žižek, on the other hand, there is no beyond of being which inscribes itself into the order of being; there is just the order of being itself. The underlying philosophical choice, writes Žižek, is between Kantian transcendental finitude and Hegelian speculative infinity: "if one asserts the non-All (ontological incompleteness) of reality," then "an Event is irreducible to the order of Being (or to a situation with regard to which it is an Event)—*it is also in-itself* not *just a 'fragment of being,'* not because it is grounded in some 'higher' spiritual reality, but because it emerges out of the void in the order of being" (Žižek 2009c, p. 213, emphasis added).

One problem with this Kantian antinomy between being and event is that it is not Badiou's. As Badiou writes, "I would like to insist that, even in the title *Being and Event*, the 'and' is fundamental." He continues, it "is not the opposition between the event and the situation that interests me first and foremost," indeed "the principal contribution of my work does not consist in opposing the situation to the event" but in posing the question "what can we derive or infer from this from the point of view of the situation itself" (Badiou, quoted in Bosteels 2011, p. 306). The event designates "what-is-not-being-qua-being" (Badiou, 2005a, pp. 173–4) and is therefore not submitted to the operation of the count-as-one; as "non-being" the event is supernumerary (ibid., p. 178). Another term for this non-being of being is the void. The void "is the unpresentable *point of being* of any presentation" (ibid., p. 77). The event is supernumerary but it is not *beyond* being; it emerges precisely out of the void of the order of being. Žižek's critique simply targets a straw figure here.

The subject as lack and force

What is at stake here is the nature of the limit, whether it is an internal limit in the order of being itself, as Žižek's asserts, or what he sees as an external limit between the order of being and the domain of the "Truth-Event" in Badiou. We can see this most clearly in Žižek's distinction between subject and subjectivization, as that which separates Lacan from post-Marxists, such as Badiou and Laclau.[4] Badiou's subject, the *subject of truth*, only emerges post-event through a truth procedure and thus, according to Žižek, fails to take into account the distinction between subject—as lack, gap, void, nothingness—and subjectivization as a process of interpellation. Therefore, it is secondary to the subject as lack. For Lacan, the subject prior to subjectivization "is the pure negativity of the death drive prior to its reversal into identification with some new Master-Signifier"

(Žižek 1998, p. 257). The subject is simultaneously the ontological gap in the symbolic order and that which comes to fill the gap:

> *"Subjectivity" is a name for this irreducible circularity, for a power which does not fight an external resisting force (say, the inertia of the given substantial order), but an obstacle that is absolutely inherent, which ultimately "is" the subject itself.*
>
> *(Žižek 1999, p. 159, emphasis in the original)*

The subject's endeavor retroactively to fill the gap sustains and generates the gap itself. Badiou refuses this identification of the subject with the gap and thus, according to Žižek, restricts the contingent act to a moment of decision, the moment of subjectivization. From Žižek's perspective, the whole Kantian opposition within Badiou of the universal order of being and the contingent excess that punches a whole in this universal order is a false dichotomy: "the subject is the contingent emergence/act that sustains the very universal order of Being" (Žižek 1999, p. 160). In other words, the subject is a paradox, the particular element that sustains the universal order.

Žižek, however, completely ignores Badiou's critique of the Lacanian subject, a critique that will later be reformulated but not completely abandoned. *Theory of the Subject*, Part V, is devoted to the dual processes of "subjectivization" and "subjective process." Both processes can be found in Lacan. The former obeys the logic of the signifier and the structural law of lack, and it can be found in Lacan's work up to the mid-1960s. The latter is governed by the topological logic of the Borromean knot, the real as excess and consistency, and can be found in his work post-1968.

Badiou diverges from Lacan in two respects: first, he insists that the real confers on the subject a degree of consistency; and second, that Lacan does not have a conception of *force*. The subject emerges out of the crossing of these two operations or temporalities; subjectivization is an interruption of the state of things and is distinguished from the subjective process through the anticipation of its own certainty. The subjective process operates *après-coup* to confer consistency on the effects of subjectivization: "the subjective process amounts to the retroactive grounding of the subjectivisation in an element of certainty that the subjectivisation alone has made possible" (Badiou 2009b, p. 251). The subject is the product of this dialectical division of destruction and recomposition, of Lacan's structural law of lack, the empty place and the excess of the real which exceeds this place. As Badiou writes:

> The subject proceeds from a subjectivisation by forcing the empty place, which a new order grounds retrospectively *qua* place, by having occupied it ... Any splace [the place of the subjective] is thus the after effect or *après-coup* of the destruction of another. Subjectivisation is the anticipation whose structure is the empty place; the subjective process, the retroaction that places the forcing.
>
> *(Badiou 2009b, p. 264)*

The subject *is* the splace, which comes from what has been destroyed. As Bosteels puts it, the appearance of a new structure, in which a subject not only occupies but exceeds the empty place in the old structure, results in the first becoming obsolete (Bosteels 2011, p. 75). Badiou, then, maintains a distinction between subject and subjectivization. His subject is at once the empty place and that which comes to fill the place. What differentiates Badiou's subject, however, is that the real confers on the subject a degree of consistency that allows it to reconfigure the consequences of its initial act of destruction.

In *Logics of Worlds* Badiou reaffirms the dialectic of the *splace* he outlined in *Theory of the Subject*. What is new in the later book, he argues, is an "entirely original theory of the subject-body" (Badiou 2009a, p. 99). The contemporary *doxa* is that "there are only bodies and languages" (ibid., p. 1), a doxa that Badiou names "democratic materialism" and rejects because it reduces humanity to a form of animality or bioethics. To be sure, the human is an animal species for Badiou; we have a biological, physical, substrate but an animal is a mortal being, it lives, it survives and it dies. To be a subject in Badiou's sense is to be immortal, it is to refuse the status of the victim, to reject mere survival and transcend our particular situations. To *think* the concept of the human is to think what lies beyond the fragility of the body, of our animal substrate, or as Badiou rather nicely puts it, a "biped without feathers," whose charms are not obvious. "Man," or the human, in Badiou's sense, is *"something other than a mortal being"* (Badiou 2001, p. 12, emphasis in the original), something other than a being-towards-death. It is in this sense that we can understand Badiou's rejection of the current emphasis on human rights as too limiting; they amount to little more than rights against death, the rights to survival against abject misery. The rights of man proper must be the rights to immortality, the affirmative rights to infinity against the contingency of suffering and death that defines our animal status.

Against this "Western" notion of democratic materialism Badiou opposes the materialist dialectic and the proposition that "there are only bodies and languages, except that there are truths" (Badiou 2009b, p. 4). The "except that" in this proposition *"exists* qua subject" (ibid., p. 45)—that is to say, if a body is capable of producing effects that exceed the hegemony of body-languages then this body will be said to be *subjectivated*, it becomes a subjectivized body or body-of-truth. Truths, in Badiou's sense, are incorporeal bodies, languages devoid of meaning, generic infinities, they emerge and remain suspended between the void and the event; in short, "truths exist as exceptions to what there is" (ibid., p. 4). Insofar as a truth has no substantial existence, it insists as an exception to what "there is." The subject of truth is also, in Žižekian terms, not a substance, "to the extent that it is the subject of a truth, a subject subtracts itself from every community and destroys every individuation" (ibid., p. 9). This notion of the subject or subjectivizable body is what is at stake in *Logics of Worlds*.

According to Badiou, there are three dominant forms of the subject today: the phenomenological or descriptive; the moral or normative; and the ideological or critical. For Badiou, however, a theory of the subject must be axiomatic in the sense that a subject affirms itself. If truths exist then there must be an active identifiable form of their production; this *form* is the subject, and as such it cannot be empirically verified. Thus, any theory of the subject is formal in the sense that "subject" designates a system of forms and operations, which involves the support of a body, a theory of operations or figures and of destinations or acts. The outcome of this operation is the production of specific types of subject: the faithful subject (who maintains a fidelity to truth and is nothing less than the activation of the present of the truth (Badiou 2009a, p. 72)). The reactive subject (who denies the truth, Badiou cites his old adversaries the "new philosophers" of the 1970s as exemplary here) and obscure subject (who occludes the truth, here we could cite all forms of religious fundamentalism). For Badiou, then, the subject is a rather rare occurrence that emerges in relation to a truth procedure, the Subject of Truth.

Žižek's response to Badiou's theory of the subject-body is to restate the now familiar criticism that what Badiou lacks is a proper understanding of the death drive. We should add to Badiou's triad of Being/World/Event, notes Žižek, a fourth term, that is to say, the "night of the world" or death drive:

> Badiou distinguishes man qua mortal "human animal" from the "inhuman" subject as the agent of a truth-procedure: as an animal endowed with intelligence and able to develop instruments to reach its goals, man pursues happiness and pleasure, worries about death and so on; but only as a subject faithful to a Truth-Event does man truly rise above animality.
>
> *(Žižek 2012, p. 823)*

However, what happens to this distinction if we introduce the Freudian notion of the unconscious? What distinguishes humans from animals (including the human-animal) is not consciousness—we can accept that animals have some degree of self-awareness—but rather the unconscious; animals do not have an unconscious. From a Freudo-Lacanian perspective it is this that distinguishes humans from animals:

> [T]he Unconscious, or rather, the domain of the "death drive," this distortion or destabilization of animal instinctual life, is what renders a life capable of transforming itself into a subject of Truth: only a living being with an Unconscious can become the receptacle of a Truth-Event.
>
> *(Žižek 2012, p. 824)*

Freud's great insight, according to Žižek, is that not only is there no human being but there is also no human animal. Indeed, Žižek takes this a step further to suggest that there is no animal *tout court*, if by animal we mean a living being fully fitted to its environment. From its birth the human being is wrenched from its animal constraints and its instincts are denaturalized by the endless circularity of the death drive by the "undeadness" or "excess of life" (Žižek 2012, p. 824).

Politics: Wiping the slate clean

In the concluding paragraphs of the chapter "The Politics of Truth" Žižek claims that Badiou's resistance to psychoanalysis is part and parcel of his hidden Kantianism. According to Žižek, Badiou's implicit Kantianism ultimately "leads him to oppose the full revolutionary *passage á l'acte*," despite his explicit anti-Kantianism and radical leftist politics (Žižek 1999, p. 166). For Žižek, we must ultimately reject the Kantian distinction between the order of a positive knowledge of being and a wholly different order of the truth event, and embrace the radical gesture of an authentic Lacanian act, an act as the real of an object preceding naming, the real as the unnamable that eludes our grasp. Žižek initially defines an "authentic act" as that "which reaches the utter limit of the primordial forced choice and repeats it in reverse, it is the only moment when we are effectively 'free'" (Žižek 1992, p. 77). An authentic act pushes beyond the limits of the social, realizing what Lacan calls "the pure and simple desire of death as such" (Lacan 1992, p. 282).

This definition raises a number of issues for a *politics* of the act, as it is an individual ethical gesture rather than a collective political response. Indeed, Žižek's two favored examples of authentic acts are suicide and terror, and his repeated exemplars are Antigone, Sethe from Toni Morrison's novel *Beloved*, and Bartleby—that is to say, individuals who act alone in order to achieve a form of subjective destitution. In *The Ticklish Subject* Žižek argues that there is no authentic ethical act without the "suspension of the Big Other," of the socio-symbolic network which guarantees the subject's identity. An act is an act of faith, it is a moment of self-authorization. Furthermore, we must distinguish between those acts that are merely performative and reconfigure the symbolic, and the "much more radical *act*" that reconfigures the entire socio-symbolic field (Žižek 1999, p. 264, emphasis in the original). The act is now conceived in terms of Badiou's event, and Žižek's examples shift accordingly from individual acts of subjective destitution to collective moments of revolutionary change such as the Paris Commune, the October Revolution and the Chinese Cultural Revolution, although, contra Badiou, he reads these events as manifestations of the death drive (Žižek 2009b, p. 196).

In marked contrast to his later enthusiasm, Žižek's initial assessment of Badiou's politics was dismissive. In "Psychoanalysis in Post-Marxism" he charges Badiou with using psychoanalysis as a "justification of failure" and using it to explain why things go wrong politically. Žižek describes Badiou's politics as a "hysterical provocation," to which he opposes "the true revolutionary stance":

> [T]he heroic readiness to endure the subversive undermining of the existing System as it undergoes conversion into the principle of a new positive Order that can *give body* to this negativity—or, in Badiou's terms, the conversion of Truth into Being.
>
> *(Žižek 1998, p. 259)*

This view was tempered in *The Ticklish Subject*, where a more sympathetic picture of Badiou's politics was presented. The fundamental lesson of postmodern politics, argues Žižek, is that *"there is no Event*, that 'nothing really happens'," and in this sense Badiou "is fully justified in insisting that—to use the term with its full theological weight—*miracles do happen*" (Žižek 1999, p. 135, emphasis in the original). Today, Žižek unequivocally endorses the slogans of Badiou's former *Organisation Politique* and has adopted many of his political positions (Žižek 2009a, pp. 118–19). There remain fundamental differences between them, however, especially with regard to questions of the party and the state, the function of negation and the place of the economy.

The major dilemma facing the left today, argues Žižek, is confronting state power when the very thought of taking over the state is seen as a redundant old left paradigm (Žižek 2009b, p. 339). The academic left today tends to conceive the primary political task as one of resisting state power by withdrawing from its scope, by "subtracting oneself from it, [and] creating new spaces outside its control" (ibid., p. 339). Žižek's conceptualization of the state, party and dictatorship of the proletariat, all filtered through Lacan's logic of "not-all," is much closer to Badiou's *Theory of the Subject* than his later work, but as mentioned above, he does not directly engage with this text.

Badiou now rejects his earlier formulation of the subject of politics as the class party (Badiou 2008, p. 37), a sequence that has exhausted itself in the sterility of the party-state couple and state socialism. The subject of politics today is the militant, who maintains fidelity to the truth of the event. The collective character of the political event opens up the infinite character of situations and "interrupts the subjective errancy of the power of the state" (Badiou 2005b, p. 145), forcing the state to reveal itself, its excess of power and repressive dimension. Contra Žižek, politics must take a distance from the state. The essence of politics "is the prescription of a possibility in rupture with what exists" (ibid., p. 24). Politics is a generic procedure, a "collective action, organised by certain principles that aim to unfold the consequences of a new possibility which is currently repressed by the dominant order" (Badiou 2008, p. 31).

Žižek draws rather different conclusions regarding the politics of subtraction, insofar as an act redefines the very horizon of what is politically imaginable, or "redefines the very coordinates of what I cannot and must do" (Žižek 2006, p. 49). Bartleby's gesture—"I would prefer not to"—is exemplary of an impotent *passage à l'acte*: "the necessary first step which … clears the ground, opens up the place for true activity, for an act that will actually change the coordinates of the constellation" (ibid., p. 342). Žižek sees in this gesture "subtraction at its purest, the reduction of all qualitative differences to a purely formal minimal difference" (ibid., p. 382). The political lesson to be drawn from Bartleby's gesture is that it "is not merely the first, preparatory, stage for the second, more 'constructive,' work of forming a new alternative order, it is the very source and background of this order, its permanent foundation" (ibid., p. 382). In other words, in a post-revolutionary situation the explosion of destructive rage is never abolished but the new situation gives body to this negativity.

The problem with Badiou's politics of subtraction—taking a distance from the state but not destroying it—is that it is a negative gesture but not a negation of the negation. It is not a determinate negation in the sense that it seeks to destroy the state. From Žižek's perspective subtraction is a negative and destructive force that becomes constructive once it has undermined the very coordinates of the system it seeks to subvert. The true art of subtraction is when the whole edifice collapses (Žižek 2009b, p. 410). What we need today, according to Žižek, is a renewed Jacobinism, a form of egalitarian terror that combines egalitarian justice, terror, voluntarism and a trust in the people (ibid., p. 461).

The weakness of Badiou's politics, as Žižek sees it, is that he is a communist but not a Marxist, and therefore has no critique of the political economy:

> [W]hile he is aware that the anti-Statist revolutionary Party politics which aimed at taking over the State apparatus is exhausted, he refuses to explore the revolutionary potential of the "economic" sphere (since, for him, this belongs to the order of Being, and does not contain potential "evental sites"); for this reason, the only way left is that of a "pure" political organisation, which operates outside the confines of the State and, basically, limits itself to the mobilisatory declarations … the only way out of this deadlock is *to restore to the "economic" domain the dignity of Truth*, the potential for Events.
> (Žižek 2006, p. 328, emphasis in the original)

Whilst it is certainly true to say that Badiou does not accord the economy the dignity of a truth procedure, he has discussed the factory as an evental site (Badiou 2006). Furthermore, until recently Žižek has also avoided any sustained discussion of political economy; indeed, his political commitments are largely limited to "mobilisatory declarations." In *The Rebirth of History* (2012) Badiou directly confronts those "friends"—his reference here is Toni Negri but the comments equally apply to Žižek—who call him a communist but not a Marxist. Badiou responds that he is perfectly aware of capitalist economics and does not need any lessons in Marxism. Contemporary capitalism retains all the features of classical capitalism and, in this sense, Marx's predictions have been fulfilled. If Marxism is reduced to the dominance of the economy, then everyone is a Marxist today, but Marxism is also about the realization of an egalitarian society, communism, and our task today is to rethink the form of political organization that can bring this about. For Badiou, this organization must be "outside time" and "outside the party." The era initiated by the Jacobins is over and we must rethink what form of political organization can articulate and preserve the generic Idea today. Badiou's critique of the party-state form offers a counterbalance to Žižek's empty invocation of the party as that which *formalizes* the revolution but does not in actual fact exist.

Sarah Kay (2003) has observed that Žižek's long-running exchanges with interlocutors, such as Ernesto Laclau and Judith Butler, often served to facilitate the refinement of concepts within his work. I believe that as much can be said for Žižek's engagement with Badiou. Tracing Žižek's critique through the categories of psychoanalysis, philosophy and politics we can see how his central concepts, such as the real and the act, have subtly changed through this encounter. Žižek's Lacanian critique of Badiou's implicit Kantianism, however, fails to engage with Badiou's early critique of the Lacanian subject and the real and, more often than not, simply restates Badiou's philosophy in Lacanese. At the same time, there has been a distinct radicalization of Žižek's politics and identification with political positions of Badiou, but again, his recourse to the party and the dictatorship of the proletariat filtered through Lacan's logic of the "not-all" fails to acknowledge Badiou's present self-critique of just such a position in *Theory of the Subject*. Žižek's engagement with Badiou has been one of the most productive, stimulating and frustrating in contemporary radical philosophy, and whatever their differences with regard to the function of repetition and negation, the real, or Kant versus Hegel, to paraphrase Badiou's remark in *Logics of Worlds*, the future is in their hands (Badiou 2009a, p. 563).

Notes

1 Žižek's first reference to Badiou in print can be found in *For They Know Not What They Do* (Žižek 1991, p. 188).
2 Lacan introduces the "myth of lamella" in seminar XI, where he describes it as "something extra-flat, which moves like the amoeba ... This lamella, this organ, whose characteristic is not to exist, but which is nevertheless an organ ... It is the libido, *qua* pure life instinct, that is to say, immortal life, or irrepressible life, life that has need of no organ, simplified, indestructible life. It is precisely what is subtracted from the living being by virtue of the fact that it is subject to the cycle of sexed reproduction. And it is of this that all forms of the *objet a* that can be enumerated are the representatives, the equivalents. The *objet a* are merely its representatives, its figures" (Lacan 1977, pp. 197–98).
3 This is exactly the same criticism Žižek makes of Judith Butler's account of sexual difference and same-sex identification (Žižek 1999, p. 275).
4 This is an argument that Žižek repeatedly levels against his opponents, especially in relation to deconstruction and discourse theory. For an early critique of Laclau along these lines, see Žižek (1990).

References

Badiou, A. (1999) *Manifesto for Philosophy*. Trans. Madarasz, N. New York: SUNY Press.
Badiou, A. (2001) *Ethics: An Essay on the Understanding of Evil*. Trans. Hallward, P. London: Verso.
Badiou, A. (2004) *Theoretical Writings*. Eds and trans. Brassier, R. & Toscano, A. London: Continuum.
Badiou, A. (2005a) *Being and Event*. Trans. Feltham, O. London: Continuum.
Badiou, A. (2005b) *Metapolitics*. Trans. Barker, J. London: Verso.

Badiou, A. (2006) The Factory as Event Site: Why Should the Worker Be a Reference in Our Vision of Politics. *Prelom* 8: 171–176.

Badiou, A. (2008) The Communist Hypothesis. *New Left Review* (II) 49. pp. 29–42.

Badiou, A. (2009a) *Logics of Worlds: Being and Event II*. Trans. Toscano, A. London: Continuum.

Badiou, A. (2009b) *Theory of the Subject*. Trans. Bosteels, B. London: Continuum.

Badiou, A. (2011) Can Change be Thought. In Bosteels, B. *Badiou and Politics*. Durham, NC: Duke University Press.

Badiou, A. (2012) *The Rebirth of History: Times of Riots and Uprisings*. London: Verso.

Badiou, A. & Žižek, S. (2009) *Philosophy in the Present*. Ed. Engelmann, P., trans. Thomas, P. & Toscano, A. Cambridge: Polity Press.

Bosteels, B. (2005) Badiou without Žižek. *Polygraph* 17: 223–246.

Bosteels, B. (2011) *Badiou and Politics*. Durham, NC: Duke University Press.

Butler, J., Laclau, E. & Žižek, S. (2000) *Contingency, Hegemony, Universality: Contemporary Dialogues on the Left*. London: Verso.

Johnston, A. (2009) *Badiou, Žižek and Political Transformations: The Cadence of Change*. Evanston, IL: Northwestern University Press.

Kay, S. (2003) *Žižek: A Critical Introduction*. Cambridge: Polity Press.

Lacan, J. (1977 [1973]) *The Four Fundamental Concepts of Psychoanalysis*, ed. Miller, J.-A., trans. Sheridan, A. Harmondsworth: Penguin.

Lacan, J. (1990 [1969]) Impromptu at Vincennes. In Copjec, J. (ed.) *Television: A Challenge to the Psychoanalytic Establishment*. Trans. Hollier, D., Krauss, R., Michelson, A. & Mehlman, J. New York: W.W. Norton.

Lacan, J. (1992 [1986]) *The Ethics of Psychoanalysis, 1959–1960, The Seminar of Jacques Lacan: Book VII*. Ed. Miller, J.-A., trans. Porter, D. London: Routledge.

Žižek, S. (1989) *The Sublime Object of Ideology*. London: Verso.

Žižek, S. (1990) Beyond Discourse Analysis. In Laclau, E., *New Reflections on the Revolution of Our Time*. London: Verso.

Žižek, S. (1991) *For They Know Not What They Do: Enjoyment as a Political Factor*. London: Verso.

Žižek, S. (1992) *Enjoy Your Symptom! Jacques Lacan in Hollywood and Out*. London: Routledge.

Žižek, S. (1996) *The Indivisible Remainder: An Essay on Schelling and Related Matters*. London: Verso.

Žižek, S. (1998) Psychoanalysis in Post-Marxism: The Case of Alain Badiou. Psycho-Marxism: Marxism and Psychoanalysis Late in the Twentieth Century. *The South Atlantic Quarterly* 97(2): 235–261.

Žižek, S. (1999) *The Ticklish Subject: The Absent Centre of Political Ontology*. London: Verso.

Žižek, S. (2004) From Purification to Subtraction: Badiou and the Real. In Hallward, P. (ed.) *Think Again: Alain Badiou and the Future of Philosophy*. London: Continuum.

Žižek, S. (2006) *The Parallax View*. Cambridge, MA: MIT Press.

Žižek, S. (2009a) *First as Tragedy, Then as Farce*. London: Verso.

Žižek, S. (2009b) *In Defense of Lost Causes*. London: Verso.

Žižek, S. (2009c) An Answer to Two Questions. In Johnston, A., *Badiou, Žižek and Political Transformation: The Cadence of Change*. Evanston, IL: Northwestern University Press.

Žižek, S. (2012) *Less Than Nothing: Hegel and the Shadow of Dialectical Materialism*. London: Verso.

5

ON THE "CRITIQUE OF VIOLENCE" AND REVOLUTIONARY SUICIDE

If the issue of the party was never fully addressed at the Essen conference, neither was the question of violence and the relationship between revolution and violence. The question of revolutionary terror and violence is probably the central issue that differentiates Žižek, and Badiou to a certain extent, from many on the left today, as he repeatedly insists on the necessity of revolutionary violence. In *The Parallax View* he notes that "in every authentic revolutionary explosion, there is an element of 'pure' violence," and it is this that liberals and the "soft" left cannot accept (Žižek 2006, p. 380). More recently, in a discussion of the relationship between the Serbian and Montenegrin national poem, *The Mountain Wreath*, and "ethnic cleansing" in Bosnia, Žižek writes that "the great divide between the liberal and the radical left concerns the question: how are we to counter this violence?" (Žižek 2009b, p. 468).

This is not only a problem for liberals, however, as Žižek's most ardent academic admirers also ignore the issue of violence in their discussions of his politics. There is no entry on violence in the indices of any of the most sympathetic books on Žižek's politics (Dean 2006; Johnston 2009; McMillan 2012). One problem that commentators have with Žižek's discussion of violence is that it is not simply a philosophical or psychoanalytic issue but centers on actual acts of violence. Unlike his Leninism, Žižek's endorsement of violence cannot be accommodated as simply a matter of formalization.

In this chapter I will address Žižek's reflections on violence through his deployment of Walter Benjamin's "Critique of Violence" and his differing accounts of the riots in France (2005) and Greece (2008, 2010). While he generally adopts a negative stance towards the violence of the banlieues, Žižek sees in Greece's riots the first step from an "abstract" or "determinate" negation that could build into something greater. From Žižek's analysis it is not clear, to me at least, what the difference between these riots is, and I turn to Badiou's analysis to articulate an alternative reading of these events. Furthermore, I want to suggest that Benjamin's conception of divine violence is not as easily reconcilable with acts of revolutionary violence as Žižek takes it to be.

Second, the radical left has been here before in the 1970s when the Red Army Faction (RAF) utilized Benjamin's "Critique" and the "Theses on the Philosophy of History" to justify their actions against the state. The RAF's campaign of armed insurrection proved to be a disaster in the 1970s and if we look at the recent upsurge of urban guerrilla groups in Greece we can see a similarly counter-productive struggle being played out. In conclusion, and taking my cue from another of Žižek's illustrations of exemplary violent resistance, the black consciousness movement in the United States in the 1960s, I want to suggest that many Marxists have a much more measured sense of the necessity of violence.

As discussed in previous chapters, in the past Žižek has written interestingly and persuasively on the break-up of Yugoslavia in terms of the Freudian notion of *das Ding* (Žižek 1990, 1993). He also, however, unapologetically endorsed the North Atlantic Treaty Organization's (NATO) military intervention against Serbia in the 1990s (Žižek 1995, 1999).[1] Today, however, his reflections on violence have moved from the fantasy structures that sustain nationalist violence to the distinction between systemic state violence and revolutionary violence. The first thing to note here is that there is nothing particularly novel about the idea of revolutionary violence or the need to distinguish between state violence and revolutionary violence in the discourse of the revolutionary left. Second, Žižek's association of terror(ism) and violence with authentic political acts is not recent. In *Enjoy Your Symptom!* Žižek defines an authentic political act as that "which reaches the utter limit of the primordial forced choice and repeats it in reverse sense," and he cites "the gesture of Gudrun Ensslin, leader of the 'Red Army Faction,' a Maoist 'terrorist' organization, who killed herself in the maximum security prison in 1978" as an example of such an act (Žižek 1992, p. 77).

What sets Žižek apart from many on the left is his insistence on "strict *egalitarian justice*" and "disciplinary *terror*" as key elements of a new form of "Jacobin-Leninist" politics (Žižek 2009, p. 125, emphasis in the original). Furthermore, revolutionary terror is not, as he insists, some kind of Stalinist aberration, but rather an intrinsic part of Marxism's historical legacy that Marxists must acknowledge. The problem today, he argues, "is not terror as such—our task today is precisely to reinvent emancipatory terror" (ibid., p. 174). Thus in an interview Žižek suggests that while the actions of the Viet Cong in chopping off the arms of children who had been vaccinated by the US Army might be "difficult to sustain as a literal model to follow, this thorough rejection of the Enemy precisely in its helping 'humanitarian' aspect, no matter what the costs, has to be endorsed in its basic intention" (Butler 2005, p. 147). Indeed! Žižek's examples of revolutionary sacrifice so often involve women and children that it is not unreasonable to ask what is going on here. Undoubtedly the use of extreme examples has a certain shock value in his ongoing polemic against political correctness and liberal sentiment, but at the same time there is a discernible macho swagger that is all too familiar in Balkan leftist politics. Furthermore, endorsing such a ruthless intention hardly amounts to a useful strategy for convincing people that the left offers a viable alternative to the systemic violence of capitalism. On the contrary, it could well play into the hands of the state as we see in Greece today where the ring-wing press locates the responsibility for the rise of racist violence from the neo-Nazi Golden Dawn party with the left. Whilst we need to vigorously reject this Cold War ideology that equates the far right with left-wing violence, the theory of the "two extremes," we also need to acknowledge that Golden Dawn's support is increasing with each act of retaliatory violence. Combating Golden Dawn through reciprocal violence, the bomb attacks on their offices by the anarchist group Conspiracy of the Cells of Fire, for example, not only does not work but appears to be enhancing their status. At the same time SYRIZA (the Coalition of the Radical Left and Movements) has consistently been forced onto the defensive as journalists insist that its leader Alexis Tsipras denounces the violence of the left. The use of violence does not necessarily challenge the state so much as legitimate its further use of violence.

Times of riot and rage

Žižek draws on Walter Benjamin's (1997a [1920–21]) distinction between mythical and divine violence in order to distinguish between the objective, systemic violence of the state and the divine violence of the revolutionary as a subjective reaction to systemic violence. Subjective violence, argues Žižek, is always sustained by two forms of objective violence: the symbolic violence embedded in language itself and the systemic violence that arises from the everyday operation of the capitalist economic and political system. Therefore, before we judge subjective violence we should first set it in the context of objective, systemic violence. It is systemic violence that provides the conditions for subjective violence and, by remaining silent on the issue, liberals and "soft-hearted" radicals are complicit in the socio-economic violence of everyday life. For Žižek, Benjamin's divine violence is precisely the direct subjectivization of this unacknowledged objective violence. Moreover, we should not dismiss too hastily sudden, "irrational" eruptions of violence that seem to come out of nowhere, as these could presage a more sustained form of engagement:

> Recent events in Europe—student protests in Greece, for example—already mark the first step in this passage from "abstract" to "determinate" negation: while they are no longer just blind acting out, many observers have noted their evident violent character as a key feature. Not violent in the sense of

killing people, but violent in the sense of disturbing public order and destroying symbolic objects of private and state property.

(Žižek 2009b, p. 482)[2]

What particularly impresses Žižek about the Greek protests is that they represent a "no" without content or concrete demands, and as such they open up "the space into which concrete demands and projects of change can inscribe themselves" (Žižek 2009b, p. 482). The protests were not an end in themselves but an excess of means over ends, an excess without end. What Žižek misses here is the entirely ritualized form that violence takes in most Greek demonstrations. The confrontation between the Black Bloc and riot police at the end of every major demonstration is entirely predictable and would appear to be a perfect illustration of what Žižek criticizes elsewhere as "pseudo-activity." In *Living in the End Times* (2010) Žižek identifies the violent demonstrations as those that followed the police shooting of Alexandros Grigoropolous in December 2008. These protests were more complex and contradictory than I can develop here, but in Thessaloniki, northern Greece, where I was based at the time, they involved at least three distinct groupings: anarchists, students and immigrants, each with very different agendas. The fact that the state restrained the police from any direct confrontation with the protestors also facilitated the continuation of violence beyond the usual night. As I argue below, I can see little that distinguishes these protests from those in France in 2005, and as such these acts only serve to legitimize state violence rather than challenge it.

Žižek appears to draw similar conclusions in his earlier reflections on the 2005 riots in Paris' banlieues:

> The Parallels with May '68 make clear the total absence of any positive utopian prospect among the protesters: if May '68 was a revolt with a utopian vision, the 2005 revolt was just an outburst with no pretence to vision. If the much-repeated commonplace that we live in a post-ideological era has any sense, it is here. There were no particular demands made by the protesters in the Paris suburbs. There was only an insistence on *recognition*, based on a vague, unarticulated *ressentiment*.
>
> (Žižek 2009c, p. 63)

Žižek characterizes these protests as "an implicit admission of impotence," the kind of pseudo-activity that we should resist (Žižek 2009c, p. 69). Resisting the hermeneutic temptation to give meaning to the riots, Žižek insists that they were essentially meaningless, a form of what Lacan called *passage à l'acte*—"an impulsive movement to action which can't be translated into speech or thought and carries with it an intolerable weight of frustration" (ibid., p. 65). At the same time, they were about visibility—an excluded group claiming the right to be recognized as citizens within the country in which they live. Žižek's discussion of the riots in

Paris and Athens certainly has a degree of analytical purchase, but the question of how we might move from this abstract negation to a more determinate one is not entirely clear. Interestingly, Žižek's dilemma regarding the issue of violence is highlighted in *Less Than Nothing*, where he suggests that violence is often "a *passage à l'acte* as a sign of impotence" (Žižek 2012, p. 298); indeed, "Violence *as such*—the need to attack the opponent—is a sign of impotence" (ibid., p. 298, emphasis in the original). In a footnote to the following page, however, he draws the "sad conclusion" that "while violence does not work, renouncing it works even less" (ibid., p. 299). Without some kind of party or organizational form, how are we to channel the demand for visibility or the impotent acting out of violent rage into something more radical and transformative? As Badiou puts it in a dialogue with Žižek, it is not enough to be negative today; we must also have affirmative proposals (Badiou & Žižek 2009, p. 81).[3]

Badiou provides an alternative reading of these events through a distinction between immediate, latent and historical riots which, I believe, introduces some clarity into the situation. An immediate riot signals unrest among a section of the population, nearly always in response to an act of state violence. It is led by the young, it takes place in a specific locality, and its demands remain indistinct (Badiou 2012, p. 22). Immediate riots are not political. At best they can pave the way for an historical riot; at worst they merely reveal the state's inability to control certain spaces. The riots in Paris in 2005 and in Athens in 2008 and 2010 are immediate riots in that they were led by young people, they were localized and they articulated no specific demands. Badiou also notes that the presence of organized crime, apparent in both the Athens riots of 2008 and 2010, is a sign of the riots' complicity with the state. An historical riot, on the other hand, indicates "the possibility of a new situation in the history of politics, without for now being in a position to realize that possibility." The uprisings across North Africa and the Middle East are thus historical riots, insofar as they represent a direct challenge to the state and articulate the demand that the existence of the masses of people who have "no existence," be recognized. The historical riot therefore has the potential to become a pre-political event, if it can coalesce around an idea. In order to produce an idea that can universalize the rioters' demands, however, a form of organization needs to be created through the work of militants (ibid., pp. 21–7). For Badiou the struggles in the Middle East had a potential for radical change that the riots across Europe lacked, albeit that potential failed to materialize in most cases. Badiou's analysis highlights the weakness in Žižek's demand-without-content. For a riot to challenge the state it must be able to universalize its demands beyond the immediate grievance. So far in Western Europe this has not been the case.

In the conclusion of *Violence* (2009c), Žižek draws three lessons concerning the nature of divine violence. First, to condemn violence outright is an ideological operation par excellence, insofar as it obfuscates and therefore colludes with systemic violence. Second, "the ultimate difference between radical-emancipatory politics and such outbursts of impotent violence is that an authentic political gesture is *active*, it imposes, enforces a vision, while outbursts of implicit violence are fundamentally reactive" (Žižek 2009c, p. 179). Third, violence is not the property of individual acts but is distributed between acts and their contexts—that is to say, between acts and activity (ibid., p. 183). In this context it is better to do nothing than to participate in localized acts of violence that only serve to help the smooth functioning of the system itself. The real threat today, Žižek concludes, is not passivity but rather the urge to do something, to be active, and to engage, when we should withdraw, step back and do nothing (ibid., p. 183). So is divine violence active or passive? How do we assess the French and Greek protests in light of this conclusion? How do we assess whether violence is imposing a new vision or simply reinforcing the status quo? For this we would need much more detailed analyses of specific situations than Žižek provides.

On the "Critique of Violence"

It is here that the deployment of Benjamin's text is crucial, as for an earlier generation of student activists and radicals in the 1960s and 1970s. Benjamin maintains a great deal of symbolic capital in the academy. To enlist Benjamin on one's own side not only ensures one's Marxist credentials but also seems to settle the argument at a stroke. However, the radical left traveled this path once before and it was disastrous, not only in its immediate consequences but for many years afterward, as the left wrestled with the legacy of the RAF, and if we are not to repeat the mistakes of the past, as Žižek warns us, then we need, once more, to return to the beginning.[4]

The question we need to address is in what sense the "Critique of Violence" can be used to justify either individual or collective acts of violence. The task of a critique of violence, for Benjamin at least, was to explicate the relationship between violence, the law and justice. At its most elementary level, argues Benjamin, within any legal system violence is restricted to the realm of means and cannot be justified in terms of ends. The question, however, remains open as to whether or not violence, as a principle, can be a moral means to just ends and in order to answer this question we must first reject the means-end dichotomy. As Benjamin writes, "a more exact criterion is needed, which would discriminate within the sphere of means themselves, without regard for the ends they serve" (Benjamin 1997a, p. 132). For Benjamin, then, the question of justice, and the "justification of certain means that constitute violence" can only be determined with reference to specific situations and from a position outside both legal philosophy and natural law (ibid., p. 134). In short, Benjamin sought to elaborate a politics of "pure means" that would break the violence of the state but this could only take place with a careful analysis of the specific violence "traced against a background of specific legal conditions" (ibid., p. 134). As Irving Wohlfarth notes, it is not possible to understand Benjamin's text without considering it within its own context. If danger and violence were key elements in Benjamin's thought it was not because he wanted to "live dangerously" in some neo-romantic way, but because he found himself caught up in shifting "constellations of danger." The context is crucial as Benjamin's work is nothing if not attuned to the temperature of the class struggle at any given moment in time and the need to improvise in the moment. The context also impacts upon our understanding of "pure violence."

In 1965 Herbert Marcuse wrote an "Afterword" to a collection of Benjamin's essays including the "Critique." Marcuse for the first time drew out the inner connections between the "Critique" of 1920 and the "Theses on the Philosophy of History" from 1940. This is a connection that the RAF would pick up on and, like Benjamin's Angel of History, insist on the necessity of blasting ourselves out of the continuum of History. What the RAF entirely ignored was Marcuse's cautionary warning that Benjamin's texts were written in a different time and context where words appear "perhaps for the last time, which can no longer be seriously uttered without taking on a false content and resonance" (Marcuse, quoted in Wohlfarth 2008, p. 15). The "Critique" was written between 1920 and 1921, at a time when there seemed to be a real possibility of revolutionary change, and violence would be necessary to avert the disaster that eventually ensued. It was the only published paper out of a cluster of projected papers on politics and violence. The "Critique" is also contemporaneous with Benjamin's theological writing, "Theological-Political Fragment" (1997b [1920–21]), and his essays on the philosophy of language.

What appealed to the RAF in the 1970s, and Žižek today, is Benjamin's rejection of the law in the name of justice, and there are certainly passages in the "Critique" that would seem to justify this reading, such as the uncompromising rejection of all liberal democratic politics as well as the rejection of politics as the art of the possible in the name of the impossible. The RAF were drawn to the "Critique" for its "'devastating' … critique of the impure, mythic violence of the state in the name of a just, divine violence and its human, namely, revolutionary counterpart" (Wohlfarth 2009a, p. 16). It is around this notion of an unknown solution or act of "pure violence" that the "Critique" turns, and everything hinges on what we understand this act of pure violence to be.

In the "Theological-Political Fragment" Benjamin observes that only "the Messiah himself consummates all history, in the sense that he alone redeems, completes, creates its relation to the Messianic" (Benjamin 1997b, p. 155). Thus, the order of the profane cannot be built on the idea of the divine; theocracy has no political meaning. The "order of the profane," writes Benjamin, "should be erected on the idea of happiness" (ibid., p. 155). As Wohlfarth puts it, the "only one valid political goal" is "to render immediate, integral, anarchic happiness possible" (Wohlfarth 2009a, p. 16). The act of pure violence that brings an end to mythic violence is the revolutionary general strike, a general strike aimed at the annihilation of state violence. The general strike is an act of violence but one which is legally circumscribed and therefore will illicit state violence if it is pushed too far. Benjamin is clear here: we must distinguish between different forms of strike, distinguishing between political strikes and the revolutionary general strike as pure revolt (Benjamin 1997a, p. 145). One does not have to endorse Benjamin's theology to see that this is not the RAF's reading of the "Critique" and that it is a rather more complex argument than reading a direct appeal to action in Benjamin's words might imply.

The question of how to distinguish between mythical and divine violence in the "Critique" is difficult to say the least. To think divine and revolutionary violence together, argues Benjamin, is to be placed between contradictory ethical demands that cannot be decided in advance but only "alone" in the "heat of the moment." The revolutionary may be released from the commandment—thou shalt not kill—but there is no legitimation for this act. The only justification is that pure profane violence is done, like its divine counterpart, for the sake of the living. For Benjamin, to be on the left is to improvise with the left hand; he urged us to seize the moment, but as Lacan has taught us the moment never comes, it is always too early or too late. Benjamin was consistently radical but in situations that constantly changed and required him to adapt radicalism. The RAF, on the other hand, transformed Benjamin's radicalism into a consistent, rigid strategy; the ends justified the means—an instrumentalization of Benjamin's ideas that runs completely counter to his thought. As Wohlfarth writes, the RAF did not put Benjamin's politics into practice but parodied them. The violence of the RAF was recognizable and therefore "impure" in Benjamin's sense. In short, the RAF did not so much blast us out of the continuum of history as continue the cycle of mythical violence, and whilst they succeeded in bringing out the full violence of the state, they did nothing to end it. Let me now turn back to Žižek and contemporary struggles in Greece.

In *Living in the End Times* (2010) Žižek appears to link the violent protests in Greece in 2008 directly to the revolutionary violence of the Red Army Faction in Germany, the Red Brigades in Italy, Action Directe in France, arguing that sometimes the masses are so totally immersed in capitalist ideological torpor that they need a wake-up call, such as direct action. "While one should reject without ambiguity," writes Žižek, "the murderous way in which this insight was enacted, one should not be afraid to endorse the insight itself" (Žižek 2010, p. 390). However, let us just consider the recent history of revolutionary violence in Greece and, again, I want to be clear here, I am talking about a specific form of violence, the idea of propaganda by deed, or punctal acts of violence that will awaken a broader mass uprising.[5]

Just over a decade ago Greece saw the demise of one of Europe's longest surviving urban guerrilla groups, November 17. N17 emerged out of the final days of military junta and the crushing of student protests at Athens Polytechnic in

1973. They were responsible for over 100 attacks on US, British, Turkish as well as Greek targets, and they assassinated 23 people. N17 combined an anti-imperialist, anti-capitalist ideology with Greek nationalism, and with their roots in the student movement and anti-dictatorship struggle there was a degree of sympathy for them on the Greek left. As with the situation of the RAF in West Germany, however, this sympathy began to wane as N17 increasingly targeted persons rather than property. At their trial the majority of members of the group renounced any kind of left ideology or political motivation for their actions.

The legacy of November 17 was quickly taken up by a new generation of revolutionaries. Revolutionary Struggle emerged in 2003 and after a fairly brief and completely ineffectual bombing campaign, the core members of the group were arrested in 2010.[6] Unlike the RAF or N17, though, Revolutionary Struggle was a rather more postmodern form of urban guerrilla group. They were anarchists and their public statements, published in a monthly satirical magazine, *To Pontiki*, seem to come down to the point that they had no demands as the state had nothing to offer them. They lacked any detailed analysis of the situation and their ideology was aimed at bringing down the state through violence.

More recently we have seen the emergence of the Conspiracy of the Cells of Fire. This group surfaced in 2008 expressing solidarity with anarchists imprisoned after the riots of the same year. Members of the group were arrested in 2009 and 2010 after a series of small-scale bombings and bank robberies. The youngest member of the group, Nikos Romanos, a friend of Alexandros Grigoropoula (the teenager killed by police in Xharchia which sparked the 2008 riots), declared himself a prisoner of war—although I am not sure of what war he is a prisoner, as the group rejects both working-class solidarity and any form of collective struggle. As an anarcho-individualist group Conspiracy of the Cells of Fire does not appear to have a consistent ideology beyond the idea that the struggle against the state is an individual affair.

Even more recently we have seen the emergence of the Group of Popular Fighters, who staged an attack on the home of the German ambassador in Athens in December 2014. In a declaration, also published in *To Pontiki*, the group claimed: "As we sprayed gunfire at the hyper-luxury home of the German ambassador we imagined beside us the thousands of people who line up at soup kitchens … the unemployed, those working for 400 euros [a month]" (Ekathimerini 2014). The Popular Fighters might well have *imagined* the massed ranks of the dispossessed alongside them as, caught in the Lacanian imaginary, the group has no links with the wider struggle against austerity in Greece. The complete lack of political analysis and increasingly the lack of any identifiable cause, coupled with a romantic individualism, is doomed to failure before it even begins. This kind of revolutionary suicide might resonate with Žižek's notion of an authentic political act or a rather literal (mis)understanding of Benjamin's "pure violence," but it will get us nowhere. As with the RAF in the 1970s, it will bring out the full force of the state's repressive apparatus but it will do nothing to further the collective struggle against inequality and injustice.

Revolutionary suicide

In *First as Tragedy, Then as Farce*, Žižek approvingly quotes the 1960s black power leader Stokely Carmichael's rejection of white society:

> We have to fight for the right to invent the terms which will allow us to define ourselves and to define our relations to society, and we have to fight that these terms will be accepted. This is the first need of a free people, and this is also the first right refused by the oppressor.
>
> *(Žižek 2009a, p. 120)*

However, we need to go one step farther, argues Žižek, and not simply find new terms by which to define oneself but to reject the dominant tradition itself and thus "deprive the whites of the monopoly on defining *their own* tradition" (Žižek 2009a, p. 120, emphasis in the original).

Whilst Žižek sees in Carmichael's position an exemplary political gesture, rejecting outright the legitimacy of white domination, Huey P. Newton (1974), the co-founder of the Black Panther Party, saw the situation slightly differently.[7] Newton clashed with Carmichael both over his race analysis and the issue of armed conflict. Carmichael insisted that given the pervasiveness of racism within North American society, the only way forward was an "armed rebellion, culminating in a race war" (Newton 1974, p. 195). Newton, on the other hand, argued for the necessity of situating racism within the context of class exploitation and the capitalist system as a whole. For Newton there was a need to build alliances and form solidarity with other oppressed groups, whatever their race. Newton concedes that Carmichael was right insofar as the white radicals destroyed the party but "he was wrong in principle" (ibid., p. 195). The Panthers, following Malcolm X's call for the founding of an African American unity movement, believed in the right to self-defense and to bear arms, as guaranteed under the US Constitution. At the same time Newton criticized "infantile leftists"—generally white leftists—who were obsessed with revolutionary violence, insisting that the party remained within the law so as not to bring upon it the full weight of the repressive state apparatus. The carrying of guns was never an end in itself and was always secondary to party organization and the support programs in the community (Caygill 2013). From this perspective the Panthers also argued for restraint, opposing spontaneous riots as these simply increased the slaughter of black people and of party members. The Black Panthers were always acutely aware that to go against the state in an armed confrontation would be futile and only result in greater losses on their side.

Revolutions, as Terry Eagleton has pointed out, are not necessarily violent affairs any more than reforms are necessarily peaceful (Eagleton 2011, pp. 179–95). I am under no illusion that the ruling class will give up without a fight, as we have seen across North Africa and the Middle East in the past few years, but Marxists have traditionally been "hostile to what they call 'adventurism' by which they mean recklessly throwing a small band of revolutionaries against the colossal forces of the state" (ibid., p. 186). For Marx, as for the Marxist Benjamin, the question of revolutionary violence is directly related to the analysis of the material forces at work in society and it is this analysis that is frequently absent from Žižek's writings on violence and is completely absent from the public statements of the new urban guerrilla groups. It is also worth recalling, as Eagleton writes, that historically the "working-class movement has not been about violence, but about putting an end to it" (ibid., p. 186). The kind of revolutionary violence we see emerging in Greece at present and at times advocated by Žižek is a complete dead end, and if we are seriously to start over again then repeating these kinds of mistakes, either theoretically or in actuality, will get us nowhere.

Notes

1   In response to a question concerning the belated intervention of NATO in the war in the former Yugoslavia, Žižek (1995) is quoted as saying: "I have always been in favour of military intervention from the West." He subsequently repeated this support, for instance in Žižek (1999): "I definitely support the bombing" of Milošević's regime by NATO.
2   Žižek has not, to my knowledge, reconsidered this statement in the light of the deaths of three young bank workers when their bank was firebombed in the general strike of 6 May 2010. These deaths resulted in a lull in the mass demonstrations and the "Black Bloc" going to ground for the following year or so.
3   Interestingly, with the anti-austerity riots extending to Slovenia with mass protests on 17 November 2012 and violent protests on 3 December 2012, Žižek remained silent on the issue. To my knowledge he has not written or spoken publicly in Slovenia in support of the protests, although he very quickly came out in support of the protesters in Bosnia-Herzegovina (Žižek 2014a, 2014b).
4   The discussion that follows draws extensively on Irving Wohlfarth's excellent three-part essay on the RAF's misuse of Benjamin's text (Wohlfarth 2008, 2009a, 2009b).
5   I am also not suggesting that this cannot happen, as it did in Tunisia in 2010.
6   The leader of revolutionary struggle, Nikos Maziotis, was subsequently released from prison as the state failed to process the case in time. He immediately went underground and committed a number of robberies but the group was largely inactive. He was caught in a shoot-out in Athens in July 2014.
7   Newton uses the term "revolutionary suicide" in a different and rather more positive sense than I am deploying it here, contrasting it to the "reactionary suicide" of those, like Eldridge Cleaver, who side with the status quo. For Newton, to become a revolutionary was to accept the inevitability of death in the name of the cause.

References

Badiou, A. (2012) *The Rebirth of History: Times of Riots and Uprisings*. London: Verso.
Badiou, A. & Žižek, S. (2009) *Philosophy in the Present*. Ed. Engelmann, P., trans. Thomas, P. & Toscano, A. Cambridge: Polity Press.
Benjamin, W. (1968 [1950]) Theses on the Philosophy of History. In Arendt, H. (ed.) *Illuminations*. London: Fontana Press, pp. 245–255.

Benjamin, W. (1997a [1920–21]) Critique of Violence. In *One Way Street and Other Writings*, trans. Jephcott, E. & Shorter, K. London: Verso.

Benjamin, W. (1997b [1920–21]) Theological-Political Fragment. In *One Way Street and Other Writings*, trans. Jephcott, E. & Shorter, K. London: Verso.

Butler, R. (2005) *Slavoj Žižek: Live Theory*. London: Continuum.

Caygill, H. (2013) Philosophy and the Black Panthers. *Radical Philosophy* 179: 7–13.

Dean, J. (2006) *Žižek's Politics*. London: Routledge.

Eagleton, T. (2011) *Why Marx was Right*. New Haven, CT: Yale University Press.

Ekathimerini (2014) Guerilla Group Claims "Anti-capitalist" Attack on German Envoy's Home. 11 February. www.ekathimerini.com (accessed 12 February 2014).

Johnston, A. (2009) *Badiou, Žižek and Political Transformations: The Cadence of Change*. Evanston, IL: Northwestern University Press.

McMillan, C. (2012) *Žižek and Communist Strategy: On the Disavowed Foundations of Global Capitalism*. Edinburgh: Edinburgh University Press.

Newton, H.P. (1974) *Revolutionary Suicide*. London: Wildwood House.

Wohlfarth, I. (2008) *Entsetzen*: Walter Benjamin and the Red Army Faction, Part One. *Radical Philosophy* 152: 7–19.

Wohlfarth, I. (2009a) Critique of Violence: Deposing the Law, Walter Benjamin and the Red Army Faction, Part Two. *Radical Philosophy* 153: 13–26.

Wohlfarth, I. (2009b) Spectres of Anarchy: Walter Benjamin and the Red Army Faction, Part Three. *Radical Philosophy* 154: 9–24.

Žižek, S. (1990) Eastern Europe's Republics of Gilead. *New Left Review* (I) 183. pp. 50–62.

Žižek, S. (1992) *Enjoy Your Symptom! Jacques Lacan in Hollywood and Out*. London: Routledge.

Žižek, S. (1993) *Tarrying with the Negative: Kant, Hegel and the Critique of Ideology*. Durham, NC: Duke University Press.

Žižek, S. (1995) Reflections of Media and Politics and Cinema. Interview with Lovink, G. *InterCommunication* 14. www.lacan.com/zizek-reflections.htm (accessed 15 July 2014).

Žižek, S. (1999) The Books Interview: The Giant of Ljubljana. Interview with Mannes-Abbot, G. *The Independent*, 24 April. www.independent.co.uk/arts-entertainm ent/the-books-interview-the-giant-of-ljubljana-1089193.html (accessed 15 July 2014).

Žižek, S. (2006) *The Parallax View*. Cambridge, MA: MIT Press.

Žižek, S. (2009a) *First as Tragedy, Then as Farce*. London: Verso.

Žižek, S. (2009b) *In Defense of Lost Causes*. London: Verso.

Žižek, S. (2009c) *Violence: Six Sideways Reflections*. London:

Žižek, S. (2010) *Living in the End Times*. London: Verso.

Žižek, S. (2012) *Less Than Nothing: Hegel and the Shadow of Dialectical Materialism*. London: Verso.

Žižek, S. (2014a) Anger in Bosnia, but this Time the People Can Read their Leader's Ethnic Lies. *The Guardian*. 10 February. www.theguardian.com/commentisfree/2014/ feb/10/anger-in-bosnia (accessed 15 July 2014).

Žižek, S. (2014b) An Open Letter to the International Community in Bosnia and Herze-govina. *LeftEast*. 13 February. www.criticatac.ro/lefteast/an-open-letter-internationa l-community-in-bosnia (accessed 15 July 2014).

6

RESOURCES OF HOPE

A critique of Lacanian anti-utopianism

In *Archaeologies of the Future* (2005), Fredric Jameson observed that postmodernism marked the end of traditional utopias, insofar as we can no longer imagine alternatives to global capitalism. For the left utopia frequently operated as code for a form of socialism that no longer seems realizable, while from the right utopianism has become a synonym for totalitarianism. What concerns Jameson is how these two views have come to overlap, today designating any form of politics that wishes to change the system radically as utopian and therefore inherently authoritarian and misguided. Yannis Stavrakakis (2007) has recently restated this position from a Lacanian perspective, arguing that utopia is a discourse that offers political solutions from the point of view of a "subject-supposed-to-know," and whose opaqueness and authority is never questioned.[1] Fascism and Stalinism are the prime examples of such utopian thought, with their imaginary promise of fullness and recapturing lost *jouissance*. What characterizes utopian thought, for Stavrakakis, is a fear of the negative, the refusal to acknowledge lack or the ultimate failure of *jouissance*. The urgent political task facing us today, he argues, is to traverse the fantasy of utopia (whether that is revolutionary, fundamentalist or post-democratic consumerist society) and reinvent transformative politics in a post-fantasmatic space (ibid., p. 261).

What has always struck me about Lacanian anti-utopianism and its critique of an obsolescent left politics is that it fails to do justice to the diversity of utopian thinking within Marxism and Critical Theory.[2] As I will argue below, Lacanians tend to generalize their critique from a specific form of utopian thought without acknowledging the significant differences between, for example, Ernst Bloch's conception of utopia as "not yet," Walter Benjamin's redemptive messianism or Theodor Adorno's reflections on a damaged life and the Freudo-Marxism of Herbert Marcuse in the 1960s, to name just some of the most obvious candidates.[3] The focus of this chapter is more specific, however. I will not address utopia in general or as a literary category but rather consider those contemporary theorists who utilize Lacan's work, again in very different ways, as a means of constructively reconceptualizing the utopian impulse.

I also take my cue from Jameson's remark that the best utopias are those that fail most comprehensively (Jameson 2005, p. xiii). Stavrakakis is right: utopia is impossible, but it is this very impulse to imagine the impossible (and fail) that marks utopian thinking today. From a Jamesonian perspective, in an era of neo-liberal austerity and when we are constantly told that "there is no alternative" (TINA), the very attempt to imagine alternative spaces, alternative ways of addressing the problem, is by definition utopian. In this sense utopia is not about visions of the "good life" or the "just society" (although there is nothing wrong in trying to imagine either), but more akin to Samuel Beckett's "you must go on, I can't go on, I'll go on" (Beckett 1979, p. 382), or Žižek's recent Beckettian slogan, "Try again. Fail again. Fail better" (Žižek 2009a, p. 86).

Far from representing a fear of the encounter with the negative, utopia often serves a negative purpose "of making us more aware of our mental and ideological imprisonment" (Jameson 2005, p. xiii). Indeed, Jameson goes so far as to argue that utopian thought necessarily carries within itself its own negation as misery, suffering and death inscribe the contradiction at the very heart of utopia; the necessary element "in order to constitute the wish fulfillment of their abolition" (Jameson 1994, p. 102). Utopian thought always contains a negative gesture, a negation of the present in the name of the impossible, and in the process it opens up the possibility for something new to emerge, for the emergence of novelty in Badiou's sense. In this concluding chapter, therefore, I will argue that it is possible to maintain a commitment to the Lacanian divided subject, the insatiability of desire and the failure of *jouissance* within an overall utopian perspective through the work of Jameson, Žižek and Badiou. Before turning to this diverse body of work I will consider the basis for anti-utopianism with respect to Lacan's own texts.

Lacan and utopia

Stavrakakis's critique of utopia is certainly not without foundation in Lacan but, as Adrian Johnston has noted, the term utopia rarely occurs in Lacan's work:

> Over the twenty-seven year course of the Seminar, Lacan directly mentions the notion of utopia a mere four times. In the fifth seminar, he associates utopianism with the aspiration toward a society organized around the communist principle "from each according to his ability, to each according to his needs" ... [H]e then indicates that this communist-utopian aspiration fails to take into account structures revealed by psychoanalysis in its treatment of the libidinal economy and subject formation. These structures (specifically those

delineated by Lacan in terms of his need-demand-desire triad) purportedly render any such utopia ... an unattainable fantasy-ideal ... [I]n the seventh seminar, Lacan ... [called] utopia a "dream world" that overlooks "the distance that exists between the organization of desires and the organization of needs" ... Freudo-Marxists of the Frankfurt School neglect precisely this gap separating desire from need ... and thereby avoid confronting those aspects of subjectivity that would be resistant to embracing easily the benefits of a revolutionary new political economy in which goods are distributed more equitably.

(Johnston 2008, pp. 72–3)

The final two references appear in seminar 16, the seminar of 1969 immediately following the revolutionary upheavals of May 1968. In this seminar, Lacan identifies both the inherent limit of the utopian imagination (in the sense that it aspires to an ideal autonomous space that is non-existent), and what he calls indissoluble barriers to the concrete actualization of a certain type of utopia. With reference to Plato's *Republic*, Lacan observes how Socrates "moves back and forth between the microcosm of the soul and the macrocosm of the *polis*" in his philosophical pursuit of the essence of justice, and claims that "the utopian *Kallipolis*" (beautiful city) envisioned in this text is a disguised distortion of the microcosmic "body image" (Johnston 2008, p. 73).[4] Such an image, writes Johnston, "of embedded spheres in which microcosm and macrocosm form a harmonious, integrated whole is an untenable fantasy" (ibid., p. 74). The indissoluble barrier to the actualization of utopia is, thus, nothing less than the impossibility of *jouissance*, insofar as this unattainable enjoyment is defined as the elimination of the discrepancy between need and desire.

Lacan's critique of utopia, then, rests on the idea of utopia as a fantasmatic anticipation of *jouissance* expected which never corresponds to *jouissance* obtained. As Johnston notes though:

[T]he kind of utopia rendered unattainable by the impossibility of *jouissance* (as an actually realized state of full, undiluted enjoyment) is that of an entirely happy set of sustainable circumstances in which all serious dissatisfactions are resolved without remainder, dissolved into the placid waters of a social milieu in which the individual microcosm and the collective macrocosm are peacefully at one with one another.

(Johnston 2008, p. 74)

This may be "a certain type of utopia," but it is not the view held by most Lacanian-influenced Marxists. Indeed, as Antonis Balasopoulos (2012) has pointed out, Lacanian anti-utopianism rests on an oversimplification not only of the diversity of utopian thought within Marxism but also of the often "conflicting modes of encounter between utopianism and the political valances of Lacanian psychoanalysis" (ibid., pp. 69–70). Lacanian anti-utopianism, writes Balasopoulos, "differentiates between political theorists for whom Lacan is the principal advocate of a politically and conceptually 'radical anti-utopianism' [Laclau, Mouffe, Stavrakakis] and ones who use his work as a means of constructively reconceptualizing the utopian impulse from a psychoanalytically informed perspective [Jameson, Žižek, Badiou]" (ibid., p. 70). Furthermore, the Lacanian critique of utopia tends to erase the difference between utopia as a textual problem, with all its baggage of narrative closure in classical nineteenth-century utopias, and utopia as a speculative category—what Jameson calls the "desire for utopia." For Balasopoulos, this erasure results in the construction of a fantasmatic enemy, a caricature of utopian thought that owes more to stalwarts of Cold War liberalism such as Popper and Talmon than it does to Lacan (Balasopoulos 2012, p. 75). As Jameson points out, the Lacanian critique of utopian thought rests on a homology between the "lacking" subject and an incomplete social, and there is no particular reason why we need to accept this homology as given (Jameson 2005, pp. 191–92). One can, as figures such as Jameson, Žižek and Badiou demonstrate perfectly well, accept the truth of the Lacanian divided subject and at the same time maintain a strong utopian impulse towards social transformation, without believing that this will result in a harmonious, conflict-free, post-ideological world.[5] The problem with rejecting all forms of utopianism is that it so often leads to a rejection of radical transformative politics in the name of the partial *jouissance* that status quo allows us. Utopia is not simply negated or discarded, notes Balasopoulos, but "is disqualified as the legitimate bearer of 'a politics of hope' or a 'politics of change,' so that these may be re-attached to an effectively utopianized version of the already extant, and increasingly repressive, institutional structures of Western parliamentary democracy" (Balasopoulos 2012, p. 75). Let me now turn to the very different uses of utopia in Jameson, Žižek and Badiou.

Jameson: Suspending the political

What Jameson defines in *Archaeologies of the Future* as the desire for utopia has long been one of his signature concerns, and here I just want to draw out some of the Lacanian roots of that desire. In an article from 1983, "Science versus Ideology," Jameson argued that Marxism reduced to a mere method of historical analysis and which does not project an alternate future, an alternate set of social relations, is worse than dead—it is utterly worthless (Jameson 1983, p. 297). Such projections (of alternative futures) are the function of ideology rather than science, and Jameson has consistently advocated the development of a properly Marxist ideology to accompany its scientific, historical method. Jameson drew on Althusser's (1984 [1970]) now familiar definition of ideology as an individual's imaginary relation to their real conditions of existence, but of more concern to me here is that behind this lay the Lacanian distinction between science and truth.

For Lacan, the subject, in its modern sense deriving from Descartes *cogito* in the field of philosophy, commenced in the seventeenth century with the foundation of modern physics and, "as an essential correlate of science" (Lacan 2006 [1965], p. 727). Modern science emerged at the same time that philosophy grounded the subject in a radical skepticism; consequently, science is founded on a fundamental division between our knowledge of the world and truth as ultimate cause. Descartes sought to anchor the subject in certainty, notes Lacan, but in doing so had to set aside the whole question of truth; as the subject can be certain of nothing except "I think," the guarantee of truth is delegated to God. Modern science, therefore, is characterized by a specific relation to truth, as Lacan puts it: "science does-not-want-to-know-anything about truth as cause" (ibid., p. 742), the truth is foreclosed from knowledge. Knowledge is produced through the chain of signifiers and must be transmissible; moreover, in being communicated it "sutures the subject it implies" (ibid., p. 744). The truth, however, is not transmissible. The truth cannot be communicated in the sense that there is no knowledge or discourse of truth. Truth is its own guarantee. For Lacan, there is no meta-language of truth:

> no language being able to say the truth about the truth, since truth is grounded in the fact that truth speaks, and that it has no other means by which to become grounded.
>
> *(Lacan 2006, p. 737)*

Psychoanalysis is a science in the sense that it is addressed to the subject of science, but it is distinct from other sciences insofar as it takes truth to be its fundamental point of reference. The fundamental paradox of the Lacanian subject is that it must assume its own causality. The subject is divided between knowledge and truth, and as Lacan writes, this is precisely "why the unconscious, which tells the truth about truth, is structured like a language," the unconscious speaks, it speaks the truth (Lacan 2006, p. 737).[6] It is this conception of the subject of science and its relation to truth that Jameson will utilize in his critique and reformulation of Althusser's theory of ideology.

In "Imaginary and Symbolic in Lacan," Jameson suggested that one problem with Althusser's definition of ideology is that it lacks any collective or class mediation, whereas the Lacanian notion of "science as a historical original form of decentring the subject" (Jameson 1982, p. 390) that does not at the same time embody the truth of the subject would seem to offer us a way forward. In the essay "Science versus Ideology" he suggested that Lacan's notion of foreclosure offered one way forward (Jameson 1983, p. 299), and in "Imaginary and Symbolic" he explored the political implications of Lacan's four discourses (Jameson 1988 [1977], pp. 113–115). A properly Marxist theory of ideology, he contends, needs to transcend the aporias of the centered subject and the indeterminate flux of the Deleuzian nomadic subject through a renewal of utopian thinking, which projects the subject to the other end of historical time, a time beyond class antagonism, alienated labor and the remorseless logic of the market. The purpose of such a displacement, however, is not a naive belief in the possibility of the utopian vision; on the contrary, it is to cast judgment on our impoverished present, through historically situating these specific forms of consciousness, the illusory centered subject and the completely fragmented subject. The ideological representation must be seen, writes Jameson:

> [A]s that indispensable mapping fantasy or narrative by which the individual subject invents a "lived" relationship with collective systems which otherwise by definition exclude him insofar as he or she is born into a pre-existent social form and its pre-existent language.
>
> *(Jameson 1982, p. 394)*

Lacan's notion of the decentered subject, structurally distanced from both language and the Real, but with an "indispensable" imaginary function, thus, offers a potential route for a Marxist theory of ideology, but one in which ideology is seen to be at one with the utopian impulse. What differentiates Jameson's conception of ideology from Althusser's is that it is mediated through the collectivity of class consciousness and is at one and the same time utopian. As he writes in *The Political Unconscious*:

> [T]o project an imperative to thought in which the ideological would be grasped as somehow at one with the Utopian, and the Utopian at one with the ideological, is to formulate a question to which a collective dialectic is the only conceivable answer.
>
> *(Jameson 1981, p. 96)*

Controversially, Jameson claims that all class consciousness, which is to say all ideology in the strongest sense of the term, is utopian insofar as it expresses a desire for collectivity.[7] Such a formulation could certainly fall under Lacan's definition of a utopia of full *jouissance*, if it were not for the fact that Jameson here deploys Bloch's distinction between compensatory and anticipatory utopias— that is to say, a utopia that compensates for contemporary ills by projecting a vision of society in which all ills are resolved (fascism) and an anticipatory utopia, which functions as an opening to the unknown (communism). The point is always for Bloch, and for Jameson, to recover the anticipatory desire from amongst the debris of our degraded present, or, as Žižek has recently come to formulate it, "to redeem the emancipator potential" from the failure of historical socialism (Žižek 2009a, p. 3).

What is new in *Archaeologies of the Future* is the idea that utopias emerge through the suspension of the political. They emerge in the calm before the storm of revolution, and they require a certain distance from political and daily life in order to be able to critique the existing order and describe the utopian moment. In this sense utopia is not a positive vision of the future so much as a negative judgment on the present:

> Its function lies not in helping us to imagine a better future but rather in demonstrating our utter incapacity to imagine such a future—our imprisonment in a non-utopian present without historicity or futurity—so as to reveal the ideological closure of the system in which we are somehow trapped and confined.
>
> (Jameson 2005, p. 46)

What is utopian today is simply the commitment to imagining alternatives as such (Jameson 2005, p. 217). Utopias come to us, as Jameson rather wonderfully puts it, as barely audible messages from a future that may never come into being (ibid., p. 54). Let me now turn to the work of Slavoj Žižek.

Žižek: "We are the ones we have been waiting for"

Žižek's reflections on utopia are rather scattered and, at first, appear inconsistent. He has not, for example, elaborated a fully developed theory of utopia in the Jamesonian sense. From these scattered remarks, however, I believe it is possible to extract a consistent view of utopia that remains grounded in Lacan and does not fall prey to the fantasmatic trap of full *jouissance*. As Stavrakakis has pointed out, in his early work Žižek endorsed a strict Lacanian anti-utopianism. In *The Sublime Object of Ideology*, Žižek dismissed utopian thinking as "a belief in the possibility of *a universality without its symptom*, without the point of exception functioning as its internal negation" (Žižek 1989, p. 23, emphasis in the original).

For Stavrakakis, it is the acceptance of the irreducibility of lack that differentiates the Lacanian left from the "utopian" left, and Žižek sadly, he argues, has fallen from the former to the latter (Stavrakakis 2007, p. 124). It was only two years after *The Sublime Object*, though, that Žižek was articulating a rather different conception of utopia. In *For They Know Not What They Do*, he writes: "utopias are 'utopian' not because they depict an 'impossible Ideal,' a dream not for this world, but because they misrecognize the way their ideal state is already idealized in its basic content ('in its notion,' as Hegel would say)" (Žižek 1991, p. 184). Utopians misrecognize the present, not in the sense that they are deluded and project impossible fantasies of the future, but on the contrary, they awaken us from the dream world of late capitalism and see things as they actually are without knowing it. In short, through misrecognition the truth of a situation is revealed.

The view of utopia as misrecognition finds echoes in Žižek's more recent work, *First as Tragedy, Then as Farce*, where he discusses the predicament of the Morales government in Bolivia, Aristide in Haiti and the Maoists in Nepal, and we might add the radical left in Greece today. The situation of these govern-ments, observes Žižek, is hopeless; the whole drift of history is against them. Objectively they will fail; all they can do is improvise in their desperation and it is this that endows them with a unique freedom and hope:

> Decried by enemies as dangerous utopians, they are the only people who have really awakened from the utopian dream which holds most of us under its sway. They, not those nostalgics for twentieth-century "Really Existing Socialism," are our only hope.
>
> *(Žižek 2009a, p. 156)*

As with Jameson's distinction between anticipatory and compensatory utopias, Žižek plays on the ambiguity of concept, elaborating the different meanings of utopia, often simultaneously—that is to say, the idea of utopia as an impossible imaginary (the harmonious society without antagonism) and the more radical sense of utopia as that which is impossible *within the framework of existing social relations* (Žižek 2009b, p. 310).

Žižek elaborated on the distinction between true and false utopias in a talk in Buenos Aires at the beginning of Astra Taylor's (2005) documentary, *Žižek!*. In an era when we can no longer imagine an alternative to global capitalism, he argued with more than an echo of Jameson, we need to reinvent the concept of utopia, but in order to do so we must first reject false utopias. Žižek outlines two false meanings of the concept of utopia: first, the old idea of an imaginary ideal society that we all know will never be realized. Second, the capitalist utopia of the realization of ever new desires that are not only permitted but even solicited in our society. In contrast to such false utopias, he suggests, a true utopia is when the situation gets so bad, when it is without resolution within the coordinates of the possible that, out of the pure urgency of survival, one has to invent a new space. Utopia in this sense is not the free play of imagination but a matter of innermost urgency as we are forced to imagine an alternative as the only way out. This is the kind of utopian thinking that we so urgently need. Žižek's reading of Lenin's explicitly anti-utopian *The State and Revolution* (1968 [1917]) as a utopian text is, I believe, exemplary of how this kind of utopian imagination might work today.

In *The State and Revolution* Lenin sought to clarify his views on the *withering away of the state* and *the dictatorship of the proletariat* against what he saw as the revision-ism and opportunism of Karl Kautsky and the German Social Democrats. The text also contains an unrelenting attack on utopian socialism and anarchism. "There is no utopianism in Marx," writes Lenin, "in the sense that he made up or invented a 'new' society" (Lenin 1968, p. 295). In contradistinction to the anarchist view of immediately abolishing the state, Lenin argues, "[w]e are not utopians, we do not 'dream' of dispensing *at once* with all administration, with all subordination. These anarchist dreams ... are totally alien to Marxism" (ibid., p. 296).

Given this explicit rejection of utopian thought by Lenin, in what sense, then, can Žižek read *The State and Revolution* as a utopian text? It was out of the experience of the complete catastrophe of 1914, when social democratic parties across Europe opted to support the war effort of their respective national governments, and facing the complete collapse of the International Socialist Movement that Lenin wrote *The State and Revolution*. Following Badiou (2005), what Žižek calls the Leninist event (the breaking of the evolutionary historicism of the second international), emerges from the recognition of "the Truth of THIS catastrophe" (Žižek 2000, p. 9, emphasis in the original). Out of this moment of despair, writes Žižek, the kernel of the Leninist "utopia" arises, "the radical imperative to smash the bourgeois state, which means the state AS SUCH, and to invent a new communal social form without a standing army, police or bureaucracy, in which all could take part in the administration of … social matters" (ibid., p. 10, emphasis in the original). The Leninist utopia arises from the recognition of utter failure and the demand for the impossible, for a complete social revolution, at a time when not even the majority of the Bolshevik party thought it possible. We should also note here that this utopian gesture is predicated upon an initial act of negation—the smashing the old state in order for the new to emerge. This is what Žižek calls an "enacted utopia":

> In a proper revolutionary breakthrough, the utopian future is neither simply fully realized, present, nor simply evoked as a distant promise which justified present violence—it is rather as if, in a unique suspension of temporality, in the short-circuit between the present and the future, we are—as if by Grace—for a brief time allowed to act AS IF the utopian future is (not yet fully here, but) already at hand, just there to be grabbed.
>
> *(Žižek 2000, p. 16, emphasis in the original)*

For Žižek, then, Lenin's utopianism resides in his misrecognition of the present (his refusal to accept the prevailing view that revolution was not possible), and consequently his ability to articulate the truth of the situation and to think beyond the horizon of the present. Lenin, writes Žižek, "stands for the compelling FREEDOM to suspend the stale existing (post)ideological coordinates, the debilitating [situation] in which we live—it simply means that we are allowed to think again" (Žižek 2000, p. 10, emphasis in the original).

In his dialogue with Judith Butler and Ernesto Laclau, Žižek defends his position against their charge of naive utopianism, insisting that today it is not the left who are utopians but right-wing populists with their dreams of grassroots democracy and belief that the market can solve all social ills. Against the predominant ideological closure which *"prevents us from imagining a fundamental social change, in the interests of an allegedly 'realistic' and 'mature' attitude"* (Butler et al. 2000, p. 324, emphasis in the original), he insists on the necessity today, more than ever, of holding the *"utopian place of the global alternative open, even if it* remains empty, living on borrowed time, awaiting a content to fill it" (ibid., p. 326, emphasis in the original). Žižek explores the possibility of keeping open such alternative spaces in *The Year of Dreaming Dangerously* (2012), where he dissects the radical protest movements of 2011–12, the *indignados*, Occupy Wall Street and the Arab Spring, for traces of an emancipator potential beyond the existing framework. One year on, Žižek is not hopeful, with the exception of Greece (on which point I would disagree with him), but he concludes the subterranean work of dissatisfaction is still going on, the rage is building up once again, there is an overwhelming sense of blockage and in this lies hope (Žižek 2012, p. 127). The question is how this rage can be turned into a revolutionary event rather than remaining senseless violence. Here Žižek draws on the messianic utopianism of Walter Benjamin. We must read the protests as signs of the future, as fragments of a utopian future. This utopian future has also increasingly come to be identified with Alain Badiou's Idea of communism, which I will consider below. Thus writes Žižek:

> [We] should learn the art of recognizing, from an engaged subjective position, elements which are here, in our space, but whose time is the emancipated future, the future of the Communist Idea.
>
> *(Žižek 2012, p. 128)*

We must learn to identify the fragments of the utopian future in the present but at the same time "keep ourselves open to the radical potential of the future" (Žižek 2012, p. 129) as nothing is given or predetermined. Žižek goes to great lengths to stress that there is no teleology here and he explicitly rejects the evolutionary historicism present in certain traditions of Marxist and communist thought. The future is open and will come to be "only through the subjective engagement that sustains it" (ibid., p. 131). Furthermore, it is only through a subjective engagement with the struggles of the present, by adopting an engaged position, that subjects will be able to identify those fragments of an alternative future. It is only those subjects who decide to take the leap into the void who will have the desire to see the truth of an event. The time of "revealed communism," writes Žižek, is over; we can no longer assume the truth of communism's historical destiny. Today, what defines a communist "is the 'doctrine' (theory) that enables him to discern in (the contemporary version of) a 'miracle'— say, an unexpected event like the uprising in Tahrir Square—its Communist nature, to read it as a sign from the (Communist) future" (ibid., p. 131).

As with Jameson, utopia for Žižek is not a blueprint for the future, or a harmonious society of full *jouissance*, where the gap between need and desire is eradicated, but instead a thought beyond the horizon of the imaginable, a leap into the unknown. We can read signs of that utopian future in the present but, as the future is radically open, we can do so only from a subjectively engaged position. I will now consider the Idea of a communist utopia further in the work of Alain Badiou.

Badiou: the Idea of utopia

Jameson is not included in the Lacanian left and Žižek, as I mentioned above, has fallen from the Lacanian to the obsolete left, but there is one figure Stavrakakis approvingly includes in the Lacanian left whom we can also invoke here in the defense of utopia, and that is Alain Badiou.

Badiou has not, to my knowledge, written extensively or systematically on utopia although his notion of the event as a rupture with *what is*, as the creation of new possibilities within a given situation, is arguably utopian to its core. It is with the increasing centrality of the operation of the "Idea" in his work, specifically the Idea of communism, that the question of utopia has begun to arise.[8] He has also addressed the issue of utopia in his seminar on Plato's *Republic* (2007–11) and his "hypertranslation," *Plato's Republic* (2012).[9] As Badiou remarks, the general theme of his seminar on Plato's *Republic* is utopia (13 January 2010) and the need to combat the contemporary perception of utopia as an entirely pejorative term deployed in the critique of radical politics. Today, utopia is seen to be the bearer of crime and violence against the social, as Glaucon remarks in the *Republic*:

> If workers, office workers, farmers, artists and honest intellectuals have trouble believing in the power of our Idea, it's because of the well-established phony philosophers, who as flunkies of the ruling order, put a whole rhetoric at its service, heaping upon the various politics of emancipation, as these are sanctioned by philosophy in the name of the Idea of communism, their old insults: Utopia! Stale old idea! Totalitarianism! Criminal idealism!
>
> *(Badiou 2012, p. 195)*

For Badiou, the future communist society will be a society based on justice and truth and, as he elucidates throughout the *Republic*, it will only be through living a life committed to the truth that a true life can be lived (29 October 2009). Furthermore, as the proletariat has no country, the future society will be a country without borders, a country that is at once nowhere and everywhere (Badiou 2012, p. 89). Perhaps to an even greater extent than Jameson and Žižek, Badiou's understanding of the critical value of utopia is grounded in Lacanian psychoanalysis.

In the seminar of 13 January 2010 Badiou explores the relationship between utopia and the Idea. What, he asks, is this communist Idea if not utopia? Is utopia itself not the Idea? It is not that simple, however, and in his elaboration of the communist hypothesis Badiou explicitly rejects a direct equivalence between communism, in the sense that he uses the term, and utopia (Badiou 2008, p. 35). For Badiou, communism denotes a general set of intellectual representations that are actualized in very different ways, therefore communism is a regulative Idea in the Kantian sense and not a specific program (ibid., p. 35). The communist hypothesis, as opposed to the disaster of twentieth-century communism, is the Idea of equality, a classless society and the withering away of the state.

The Idea of communism does contain, however, an essential utopian component, and it is here that Badiou draws upon Lacan; utopia is the imaginary form of the Idea. The Idea is the object of an educational protocol whereas utopia is not related to the procedures of education. Utopia is rather a spontaneously circulating subjective imaginary which cannot be understood or transmitted as a specific object of educational protocols. An Idea consists of three essential components: a truth procedure, an historical dimension and a subjectivation.[10] For Badiou, an Idea is precisely "the subjectivation of an interplay between the singularity of a truth procedure and a representation of History" (Badiou 2010, p. 3). These three components of the idea also map onto Lacan's three orders: the truth procedure is the real upon which the Idea is based; History only exists for Badiou symbolically; and the process of subjectivation is imaginary. To put it another way, politics is real, history is symbolic and ideology is imaginary. Badiou deploys the real here in Lacan's sense as that which is unsymbolizable but "exists in a given world, and under very specific conditions" (ibid., p. 4). An event, therefore, paves the way for the possibility of what is strictly impossible in a situation—as Badiou writes, "an event is the occurrence of the real as its own future possibility" (ibid., p. 7).

Just as Lacan's three orders co-exist in tension with one another and each cannot function without the other two, utopia is a necessary imaginary function in order for the subject to accede to the symbolic and undertake political action. As Badiou puts it, "the communist Idea is what constitutes the becoming-political Subject of the individual as also and at the same time his or her projection into History" (Badiou 2010, p. 4). Badiou draws attention to the fact that Plato does not resort to the usual defense against accusations of utopianism, that is to deny that one is utopian, but rather embraces the necessity of false utopias, the lie at the heart of all truth, or what we may call the necessary or "true lie." Plato introduces the subject of utopia, the "true lie," into the *Republic* through the myth told by a Phoenician sailor:

> "In many countries," he said, "society is strictly divided into three social classes that hardly mix with one another. First there are the financiers, the wealthy property owners, the senior judges, the military commanders, the chairmen of boards of directors, the politicians, and the big moguls of mass media, the press, radio and television. Then there's the host of intermediate professions: white-collar workers, nurses, low-level managers, teachers, youth activity organizers, so-called intellectuals … and I could go on and on. Finally, there are the direct producers: farmers, workers, and especially those newly arrived proletarians who come in droves from the Dark Continent today. Our Phoenician mythology says that this is a natural and necessary division. It's as if god had made our country's inhabitants from a mixture of earth and metal. On the one hand, since they're all made from the same earth, they're all from the same country, they're all Phoenicians, all necessary

patriots. But, on the other hand, the metal content distinguishes them from one another."

(Badiou 2012, p. 109)

The ideological aspect of this myth is, of course, its naturalization, the natural division of society into different classes of people, but within this myth Badiou detects a counter-myth, the utopian element at the core of this ideological myth, the earth, the element that all people share in common and does not distinguish between one and another. Utopia is in this sense a counter-myth, it is distinct from the Idea and refers us to the level of collective existence. While myth naturalizes the social division of classes, the counter-myth of utopia directs us to the order of equality and justice—that is to say, the Idea of communism. As with Jameson, then, utopia for Badiou is inextricably linked to ideology, *qua* its imaginary function, it presents the counter-myth of collectivity, an idea of social organization and the abolition of private property in contrast to the "natural" division of labor. The negative or critical value of utopia is precisely that it presents us with a form of collective organization in contrast to the idea that everything that exists is natural. For Badiou, utopia dictates that society must be reconstructed, political action must be regulated and that the state must be abolished (13 January 2010). Plato's utopia, he argues, is a real utopia insofar as it is an Idea.

In this account of utopia in Jameson, Žižek and Badiou I have suggested that one can maintain a commitment to the Lacanian divided subject, as all three theorists do, and at the same time an equally strong commitment to the utopian impulse. The Lacanian critique of utopia, I have argued, is directed at "a certain type of utopia," the utopia of full *jouissance*, and from a Lacanian perspective this is an impossible Ideal image. This critique of utopian thought not only fails to acknowledge the diversity of utopian thinking within Marxism and Critical Theory but also constructs a fantasmatic figure that bears no resemblance to Jameson's desire for utopia, Žižek's enacted utopia or Badiou's Idea of utopia. In this sense, Lacanian anti-utopianism tells us more about the politics of the Lacanian left than it does about utopia, as the "pernicious fantasy" of utopia is generalized to all forms of radical transformative politics. As Lacan's response to the students at Vincennes in the aftermath of May 1968 revealed, there is just as much an inherent conservativism to Lacanian psychoanalysis as there is an emancipator potential.[11] The utopian desire, I have argued, is the desire to redeem that emancipatory potential. Jameson, Žižek and Badiou offer just a few perspectives on contemporary utopian thought and each, in their very different ways, demonstrate the critical negativity of utopianism through its demystification of the present.

As Jameson puts it, utopian thought is plagued by a perpetual reversal in which "our most energetic imaginative leaps into radical alternatives [are] little more than the projections of our own social moment and historical or subjective situation" (Jameson 2005, p. 211). As such, utopianism stands as a perpetual judgment on the present and the impossibility of imagining a more just and equitable future society. However, as with Badiou's notion of the event, utopia also directs us to the necessity of creating the possible out of the impossible, of moving beyond the negative and simply "wiping the slate clean" to some kind of affirmative propositions.

Notes

1 For a discussion of the "subject-supposed-to-know," see Lacan (1977, pp. 230–43).
2 In *The Lacanian Left* Stavrakakis identifies Trotsky as a left utopian (Stavrakakis 2007, p. 261), and in *Lacan and the Political* he criticizes an early paper of mine (Homer 1996) for its naive utopianism (Stavrakakis 1999, Ch. 4).
3 For a Lacanian critique of Marcuse's metapsychology see Stavrakakis (1999), and of his utopianism see Johnston (2008).
4 Badiou notes that whilst Lacan held a very negative view of the *Republic* we should not extend this to his view of Plato himself. Lacan read the *Republic* as a "fundamentally ironic dialogue" (Badiou 2012, p. 367, note 6).
5 This, after all, has been one of the enduring insights of Althusser's ground-breaking, although ultimately flawed, attempt to utilize Lacanian psychoanalysis for a reformulated theory of ideology.
6 It is worth noting here that Lacan does not see his definition of science as incompatible with Marxism: "The separation of powers is at least announced in Marxism, the truth as cause being distinguished from knowledge out into operation" (Lacan 2006, p. 738), or his theory of the signifier as incompatible with historical materialism, although historical materialism has left the field unexplored (ibid., p. 743).
7 See Eagleton (1990, p. 404) for a critique of Jameson on this issue.
8 See Badiou (2010, note 1) for an account of the emergence of the theme of the Idea in his work.
9 I would like to thank Daria Kunznetsova for her help in translating this seminar.
10 See Badiou (2009), *Theory of the Subject*, Part IV, for an elaboration of the process of subjectivation.
11 Confronted by students at Vincennes to articulate his position regarding their revolutionary demands, Lacan responded: "the aspiration to revolution has but one conceivable issue, always, the discourse of the master. That is what experience has proved. What you, as revolutionaries, aspire to is a Master. You will have one" (Lacan 1990, p. 127).

References

Althusser, L. (1984 [1970]) Ideology and Ideological State Apparatuses (Notes Towards an Investigation). In *Essays on Ideology*. London: Verso.

Badiou, A. (2005) *Being and Event*. Trans. Feltham, O. London: Continuum.

Badiou, A. (2007–11) *Pour aujourd'hui: Platon!* www.entretemps.asso.fr/Badiou/seminaire.htm.

Badiou, A. (2008) The Communist Hypothesis. *New Left Review* (II) 49. pp. 29–42.

Badiou, A. (2009) *Theory of the Subject*. Trans. Bosteels, B. London: Continuum.

Badiou, A. (2010) The Idea of Communism. In Douzinas, C. & Žižek, S. (eds) *The Idea of Communism*. London: Verso.

Badiou, A. (2012) *Plato's Republic: A Dialogue in 16 Chapters*. Trans. Spitzer, S. New York: Columbia University Press.

Balasopoulos, A. (2012) Varieties of Lacanian Anti-Utopianism. In Blaim, A. & Gruszewska-Blaim, L. (eds) *Spectres of Utopia: Theory, Practice, Conventions*. Frankfurt am Main: Peter Lang.

Beckett, S. (1979) *The Unnamable. The Beckett Trilogy*. London: Picador.

Butler, J., Laclau, E. & Žižek, S. (2000) *Contingency, Hegemony, Universality: Contemporary Dialogues on the Left*. London: Verso.

Eagleton, T. (1990) *The Ideology of the Aesthetic*. Oxford: Basil Blackwell.

Homer, S. (1996) Psychoanalysis, Representation, Politics: On the (Im)possibility of a Psychoanalytic Theory of Ideology. *The Letter: Lacanian Perspectives on Psychoanalysis* 7: 97–109.

Jameson, F. (1981) *The Political Unconscious: Narrative as a Socially Symbolic Act*. London: Methuen.

Jameson, F. (1982 [1977]) Imaginary and Symbolic in Lacan: Marxism, Psychoanalytic Criticism, and the Problem of the Subject. In Felman, S. (ed.) *Literature and Psychoanalysis, The Question of Reading: Otherwise*. Baltimore, MD: Johns Hopkins University Press.

Jameson, F. (1988 [1977]) Imaginary and Symbolic in Lacan. In *The Ideologies of Theory: Essays 1971–1986, Vol. 1 Situations of Theory*. London: Routledge.

Jameson, F. (1983) Science versus Ideology. *Humanities in Society* 6.

Jameson, F. (1994) *The Seeds of Time*. New York: Columbia University Press.

Jameson, F. (2005) *Archaeologies of the Future: The Desire Called Utopia and Other Science Fictions*. London: Verso.

Johnston, A. (2008) A Blast from the Future: Freud, Lacan, Marcuse, and Snapping the Threads of the Past. *Umbr(a): A Journal of the Unconscious*: 67–84.

Lacan, J. (1977 [1973]) *The Four Fundamental Concepts of Psychoanalysis*, ed. Miller, J.-A., trans. Sheridan, A. Harmondsworth: Penguin.

Lacan, J. (1990 [1974]) Impromptu at Vincennes. In Copjec, J. (ed.) *Television: A Challenge to the Psychoanalytic Establishment*. Trans. Hollier, D., Krauss, R., Michelson, A. & Mehlman, J. New York: W.W. Norton.

Lacan, J. (2006 [1965]) Science and Truth. In Fink, B. (trans.) *Écrits*. New York: W.W. Norton.

Lenin, V.I. (1968 [1917]) The State and Revolution. In *Selected Works*. Moscow: Progress Publishers.

Stavrakakis, Y. (1999) *Lacan and the Political*. London: Routledge.

Stavrakakis, Y. (2007) *The Lacanian Left: Psychoanalysis, Theory, Politics*. Edinburgh: Edinburgh University Press.

Žižek, S. (1989) *The Sublime Object of Ideology*. London: Verso.

Žižek, S. (1991) *For They Know Not What They Do: Enjoyment as a Political Factor*. London: Verso.

Žižek, S. (2000) Repeating Lenin. www.lacan.com/replenin.htm (accessed 1 July 2010).

Žižek, S. (2009a) *First as Tragedy, Then as Farce*. London: Verso.

Žižek, S. (2009b) *In Defense of Lost Causes*. London: Verso.

Žižek, S. (2012) *The Year of Dreaming Dangerously*. London: Verso.

Filmography

Žižek! (2005) Film. Directed by Astra Taylor. [DVD] USA/Canada.

INDEX

114 Index